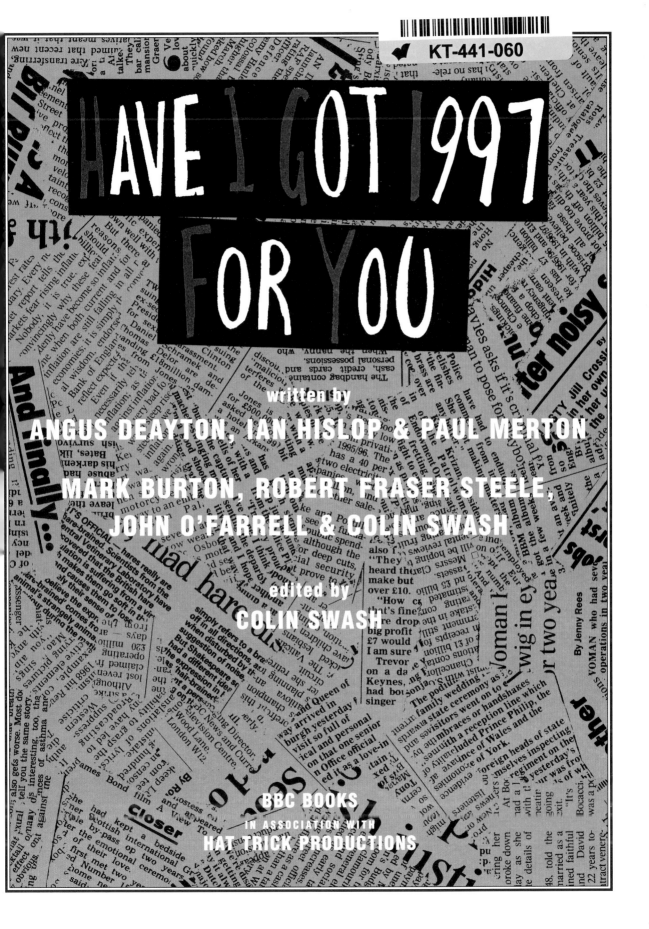

HAVE I GOT 1997 FOR YOU

written by

ANGUS DEAYTON, IAN HISLOP & PAUL MERTON

MARK BURTON, ROBERT FRASER STEELE, JOHN O'FARRELL & COLIN SWASH

edited by

COLIN SWASH

BBC BOOKS
IN ASSOCIATION WITH
HAT TRICK PRODUCTIONS

30 Monday

31 Tuesday

New Year's Eve
Up and down the country, the British people flock to pubs and clubs in record numbers, as Angus sees in the New Year on BBC1.
Birthday – Alex Salmond MP (b.1954)

SNP leader, Alex Salmond, a stubborn single-issue politician with a chip on his shoulder about the English. (That's except for Scottish readers, for whom he is a pertinent and witty statesman with an interesting slant on the devolution issue.)

1 Wednesday

New Year's Day
Anniversary – UK joins the European Economic Community (1973)
A bleak day, marked every year by Eurosceptic MP Sir Teddy Taylor, with a one minute silence and 23 hours, 59 minutes of talking.

John Major's a very nice man, but I may have to vote against him on Europe. You know, there was this story just the other day about a brass plate company in Italy that gets 1.7 million lira just for delivering non-existent fruit juice to NATO headquarters in Palermo, honestly, I'm not anti-French or anti-German, I'm just against the EC, I mean, believe it or not, we are actually having to spend money destroying 132 tonnes of cauliflowers...

*Yes, but we just want you to destroy **one** cauliflower.*

Thursday 2

Anniversary – King Zog of Albania deposed (1946)

King Zog, removed from the throne, 2nd January 1946. A lousy start to the year.

Friday 3

Saturday 4

Birthday – Arfur the London Zoo lion (b.1989)

In 1993, a homeless 'Care in the Community' patient was mauled by Arfur whilst trying to get into his cage. He has since been given round-the-clock counselling and top-class medical care, while the patient has been shoved back on the streets with a bottle of tranquillizers.

Sunday 5

❝Seize the day; trust the morrow as little as possible.❞

⑥ Monday

Birthday – Angus Deayton (b.1956)

Angus, aged 7 months

Rowan Atkinson (b.1955)

Terry Venables (b.1942)

Joan of Arc (b.1412)

Angus, aged 13

IT'S FASCINATING to think that had I been born one year earlier I might have been Mr Bean, 13 years earlier and I might have been manager of the England football team, and 544 years earlier and I might have been burnt alive in a hideous medieval execution. Fortunately for me I was born in 1956 in Surrey, where most forms of execution had, by that time, been outlawed – with the sole exception of 'drawing and quartering' which was still standard for certain minor parking offences.

My best ever birthday cake was in 1969, when my mother baked one in the shape of a Subbuteo pitch – the only drawback being that it was so good I did actually use it as a Subbuteo pitch until 1974, when it was decided that the smell of rotting sponge cake emanating from my bedroom was just too disgusting.

AT THE AGE of 17, as you can see from this photograph...

MY EARLIEST memory of a birthday present is this yellow and blue tricycle. In fact I'd had my heart set on a BMX mountain bike, but my mother explained to me that they hadn't been invented yet. Anachronistic hypotheses are a tricky concept for a 4-year-old but I realised it was all part of the learning process.

... one of my presents was an absurd wig and beard. Still, as it was a gift, I felt duty-bound to wear it for six years before getting rid of it. My main present that year though, pictured behind me, was Ben Nevis – given to me by a rich uncle. Unfortunately, I'd already been given Sca Fell Pike by someone else, but luckily I was able to take it back and change it for a BMX mountain bike, which by this time had been invented.

Sadly, birthdays are not what they were.

A YEAR LATER, as you can see, my father's present to me was to erect a Chinese water torture in the back garden. This was before the days of 'children's entertainers' and we very much had to make our own fun. This involved a variety of party games; there was the 'eating too many Smarties and being sick' game, the 'beating up the small boy in spectacles' game and my personal favourite, the 'knocking the most valuable ornament off the mantlepiece and watching it smash on the fireplace' game.

THIS WAS THE HIGH-SPOT of my most recent birthday last January, just as things were really hotting up. I hadn't actually met any of the three people who turned up, but it was very good of them to stay till half past three and help drink the contents of my fridge.

 Manners require time, as nothing is more vulgar than haste.

7 Tuesday

Why not celebrate
Arthritis Education Week
by subscribing to
arthritis|news ?

If you want to keep abreast of all the issues relating to the painful inflammation of human joints, this journal is an absolute must. Though admittedly, that's quite a big 'if'.

8 Wednesday

Birthday – Elvis Presley (b.1935)

The King of Rock'n'Roll, whose tragically premature death, brought on by sustained over-eating and drug abuse, is of little medical interest to arthritis sufferers.

9 Thursday

Anniversary – The Introduction of Income Tax (1799)

Income tax, at a rate of two shillings in the pound, was introduced to fund the Napoleonic Wars by Prime Minister William Pitt the Younger, son of Pitt the Elder, whose father in turn was Pitt the Even Elder, who was himself son of Pitt the Ridiculously Old, or Pitt the Dead, as he later became known.

Seven years after introducing income tax, Pitt the Younger died from a heart attack. Not arthritis.

Friday 10

Margaret Thatcher Day (Falklands)

'Thatcher Day doesn't mean such a lot. There aren't any fireworks or anything.'
SPOKESMAN, FALKLAND ISLANDS GOVERNMENT

'It's a public holiday, that's all.'
SPOKESWOMAN, FALKLAND ISLANDS COUNCIL,
'Oh, hang on, it's not even a holiday.'

Apparently, Mrs Thatcher was so proud of her role in the Falklands campaign, that on a tour of Chequers with Andrew Lloyd Webber, she pointed out a chair, saying, 'This is the chair I sat in when I decided to sink the Belgrano.' The chair was facing in a south-westerly direction and was said to be 'no threat to the desk.'

Lady Thatcher herself has recently experienced severe arthritic pain in her fingers, which will perhaps come as some comfort to a lot of arthritis sufferers. And a lot of non-sufferers.

Saturday 11

Anniversary – Enver Hoxha confirms exile of King Zog and proclaims Albania a republic (1946)

Anniversary – Albanian premier Mehmet Shehu dies during a dinner-party shoot-out involving Enver Hoxha (1982)

Enver Hoxha, no friend of Zog's.

Mehmet Shehu, no friend of Hoxha's.

Sunday 12

Arthritis Education Week ends

More importantly, the *Have I Got News for You* team loses their copy of *Albania – the Facts*.

❛ Look not a gift horse in the mouth. ❜

13 Monday

14 Tuesday

Anniversary – Humphrey Bogart (d.1957)

Bogart died whilst married to his fourth wife, Lauren Bacall. The film of his life story was abandoned when Hollywood moguls said no-one would want to see a movie called *Four Weddings and a Funeral*.

Bogart's third wife Mayo once flew into a rage, slashed her wrists, set fire to the house and stabbed him with a carving knife. That was the last time he ever left the toilet seat up after going to the loo.

15 Wednesday

16 Thursday

○ Full moon.

17 Friday

● Or is it a full moon *tonight*? Hard to tell, really.

18 Saturday

○ ● Could be a full moon or a new moon. To tell the truth, the computer's gone down.

19 Sunday

○ ● Snookered on the pink

20 Monday

○ ● Yes!

Tuesday 21

THE DOOR'S ALWAYS OPEN FOR MILITANT RAMBLERS

Militant ramblers have asserted their right to use an ancient footpath in Westbury, Wiltshire, even though a house has been built on top of it. Because the house was built without official planning permission, the owners are now legally obliged to let absolutely anyone come through the front door. They say they don't mind the odd rambler wandering in, but it's hard to concentrate on the telly when the fox hunt comes through.

Wednesday 22

○ ● This for the match.

Thursday 23

● In off. Bugger.

Friday 24

Saturday 25

Birthday – Emma Freud (b.1962)

Emma Freud is rhyming slang for 'haemorrhoid', just as Richard the Third is rhyming slang for 'bird', and Gareth Hunt, quite obviously, isn't. Emma comes from the family that produced Sigmund Freud, the father of psycho-analysis, Sir Clement Freud, Member of Parliament, and Esther Freud, the award-winning novelist. Not to be outdone, Emma took over Gary Davies' show on Radio 1.

Sunday 26

Australia Day

A bank holiday in Australia – though quite why anyone who buys a diary in the UK needs to be reminded of when people on the other side of the world are having a day off is a mystery.

❝ March in Janiveer, Janiveer in March, I fear. ❞

BBC NEWS JUST IN

After reports of contamination in the farmland around Sellafield, the man from the Ministry gives the area the all-clear.

At the important American Land Rights Conference, disaster strikes for Chief Sitting Bull, when the wind suddenly changes direction.

In London, a royal equerry's career is ruined, when he's caught thinking 'Nice arse'.

A car wash firm in Marlow denies that there's a problem with the 'Extra Hot' setting.

... and rumours rock the Conservative Party that Gyles Brandreth may have fathered a love-child in Australia.

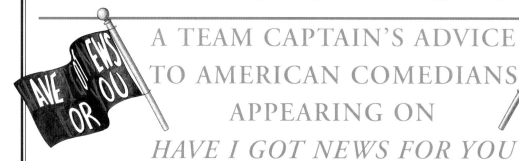

A TEAM CAPTAIN'S ADVICE TO AMERICAN COMEDIANS APPEARING ON *HAVE I GOT NEWS FOR YOU*

DURING THE SHOW

• Do insult the Queen Mother. British people hate her and love a good laugh at her expense.

• David Mellor is universally loved. Indicate that you are a friend of his at an early point in the show.

LOVE

HATE

• Muslims are the most tolerant of this country's minorities. A joke about Islam is a sure winner.

• Gaby Roslin is the British equivalent of David Letterman. Ring her before the show for some topical gags.

• John Major is known as 'The Iron Lady'. Use this to show off your inside knowledge.

• 'Fanny' in England just means 'bottom'. Always use it.

THE PANEL

■ Angus Deayton is known for his brown suites. He has a huge house in Mayfair full of brown suites. 'Brown suites' is one of the show's catchphrases.

■ Paul Merton is married to Mrs Merton, the comedienne who is actually a man in drag called Dame Edna Everage. Mention this to get Paul on your side.

■ Ian Hislop is supposed to look like the newsreader Julia Somerville. Point this out.

AFTER THE SHOW

Once you have lost the quiz to Paul and his guest, you will be invited upstairs to hospitality by someone calling himself a producer. You must say no. In England, a 'producer' is a transsexual prostitute and their attempts to seduce and then mug American comedians have become a national scandal. Leave the building immediately and go for a pleasant evening's sightseeing.

England is famous for its doubledecker taxis. To hail a taxi, simply step out into the road in front of it. The driver will take you wherever you want.

If you wait long enough, the magnificent dome of St Paul's Cathedral will rise to make room for tall ships passing through.

For a taste of British culture, every American should pay a visit to Her Majesty's Theatre – Shakespeare's birthplace.

There's no better way to round off your stay in England than to pop into Big Ben, home of popular news-reader Trevor McDonald.

Nelson's Column, London's famous monument to Nelson Mandela. It's considered good luck to climb the column and dive into the fountain below.

Have a nice day !

27 Monday

Anniversary – John Logie Baird gives the first public demonstration of television (1926)

28 Tuesday

First viewer writes in to complain (1926)

29 Wednesday

Birthday – Germaine Greer (b.1939)

In 1995, Germaine Greer accused a fellow feminist of having bird's nest hair, showing off three fat inches of cleavage, and wearing 'fuck-me' shoes.

That's actually incorrect. I was just talking about the self-image of some women being so low... I didn't actually name anybody.

This was in a piece about Suzanne Moore, though, wasn't it?

Why would shoes want to be fucked anyway?

What sort of shoes are YOU wearing, Germaine?

Don't-fuck-me shoes. Leave-me-alone-or-I'll-kick-you-in-the-face shoes.

Just checking.

Can you get fuck-me socks? You open up your present on Christmas Day and say, 'fuck me, socks!'

Germaine Greer was romantically linked with Jonathan Aitken back in his bachelor days. Despite being aware of his right-wing views, she couldn't resist him in his dark grey suit, his Eton tie and his fuck-me Hush Puppies.

30 Thursday

Greer Footwear Plc unveils the Fuck-Me Shoe.

Friday 31

The directors of TCP hold an emergency meeting about how Gargling Week has led to their product sharing a page with a torrent of four-letter words. Whole of marketing department is sacked.

❛ There's many a slip twixt cup and lip. ❜

1 Saturday

Birthday – Boris Yeltsin (b.1931)

After landing at Shannon Airport, Boris Yeltsin kept the Irish Prime Minister waiting for him on the tarmac for over an hour. Yeltsin's doctors explained that he'd been unable to leave the plane as there was still some alcohol on board.

2 Sunday

3 Monday

Birthday – Val Doonican (b.1929)

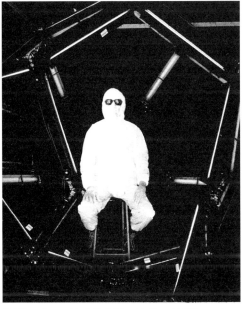

Val Doonican adds Sellafield to his list of 1997 tour dates.

4 Tuesday

5 Wednesday

Birthday Douglas Hogg MP (b.1945)

Douglas Hogg used to be a Special Constable, although it's not clear if he used his police training in the European Commission discussions over British beef. All we know is that the ban was partially lifted and Jacques Santer confessed to the Birmingham pub bombings.

6 Thursday

7 Friday

Chinese New Year – The Year of the Ox

'I think this is going to be my year.'

ODD | ONE | OUT

MONA LISA

DEEP SEA ANGLER FISH

TERESA GORMAN

A KLINGON

ANSWERS

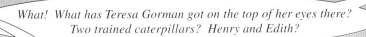

*The Klingon's forehead is turning into a Cornish pastie.
And that makes him an odd man out, surely, in any crowd.*

Yes, the Odd One Out is the Klingon, as none of the others have eyebrows.

*What! What has Teresa Gorman got on the top of her eyes there?
Two trained caterpillars? Henry and Edith?*

They're two tattoos.

*Tattooed eyebrows? How do we know that's not a tattooed face?
She might be someone completely different underneath.
She might be John Gummer.*

*T*he answer is that none of them have eyebrows, with the exception of the Klingon, who appears to be almost entirely eyebrow.

*K*lingons are now so popular that there are Klingon-speaking societies for people to dress up as Klingons and use phrases such as: 'Surrender or die' and 'Beam me up'. Although, so far, there's no Klingon phrase for 'Get a life'.

A seventeenth-century restorer inadvertently scrubbed off a number of the Mona Lisa's features, one of which being her eyebrows. The others, of course, being her handlebar moustache and West Ham bobble hat.

*T*he Deep Sea Angler Fish hasn't got any eyebrows, although, on a positive note, it hasn't exactly ruined its appearance.

*A*s a teenager, Teresa Gorman plucked out her real eyebrows. Since then, she's had some new ones tattooed onto her face – although her husband managed to dissuade her from having 'Essex Skins' tattooed on her forehead.

*Did Teresa Gorman just stop at plucking her eyebrows,
or was it all the body hair?*

I don't actually know her that well, Paul.

*Lower down, you might have a tattoo of the
Spanish Armada. Coming into port. Sailors at the side, whistling.
Hot dog stand, you could have the lot.*

Thank you, that's a lovely image.

TRAINSPOTTER'S GUIDE II

EVER SINCE THE PUBLICATION of the first *Have I Got News For You* Trainspotter's Guide*, hundreds of letters have poured into the production office about other things. Trainspotters, obviously, are too busy out spotting trains. Still, we've gathered a whole load of new statistics and the *Economist* has refused to print them, so here they are anyway.

As this chart shows, Ian's record of consistent failure is not so dramatic when compared to the rate of inflation.

However, any shareholder investing in Paul would have seen a sixfold return on their initial outlay, three times the value of the Government's much-heralded TESSA scheme. This has led to stock market speculation that Paul may be the subject of a takeover bid from British Aerospace. According to the Financial Times TV critic, the combination of Britain's foremost exporter of weapons of death and a lovable comedy quiz king would be the small investor's dream. Ian, on the other hand, requires considerable fattening up before privatisation.

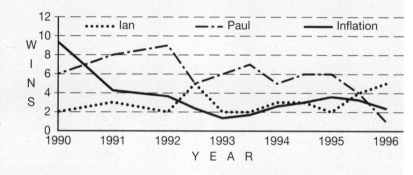

This bar chart offers a breakdown of the two captains' performance on a series-by-series basis.

As you can see, the very real possibility exists that, if Paul were to win a series 10–0, Canary Wharf would no longer be the tallest building in Britain.

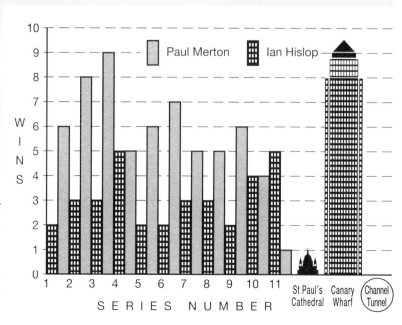

---

*to be found in *Have I Got News For You, the Shameless Cash-In Book* – still available in good bookshops, price £6.99, £5.99 or, if you find the right bargain bin, 49p

RESULTS UPDATE
Series VIII – XI

1	Mohammed Al-Masari	59.09%	22=	Julian Clary	35.00%	43=	Hugh Dennis	24.98%
2	Gordon Kennedy	55.55%		Alan Cumming	35.00%		Michael Buerk	24.98%
3	Richard Wilson	55.00%	24	Eddie Izzard	34.31%	45	Lee Hurst	23.61%
4	Nick Hancock	54.54%	25=	Bob Mills	33.33%	46=	Teresa Gorman MP	22.73%
5=	Germaine Greer	50.00%		Tim Rice	33.33%		David Icke	22.73%
	Fred MacAulay	50.00%		Jack Docherty	33.33%		Alexei Sayle	22.73%
7	Paul Merton	47.27%	28	Claire Rayner	31.82%	49=	Terry Major-Ball	22.22%
8	Sir Teddy Taylor MP	45.82%	29	Hattie Hayridge	30.76%		Paula Yates	22.22%
9	John Bird	45.68%	30	John Fortune	30.14%		Mark Little	22.22%
10	Michael Winner	44.44%	31=	Diane Abbott MP	30.00%	52	Martin Clunes	21.59%
11	Melvyn Bragg	43.75%		Charles Kennedy MP	30.00%	53	Helen Atkinson-Wood	20.83%
12=	Craig Charles	41.65%	33	Clive Anderson	28.89%	54	Dermot Morgan	20.00%
	Judge James Pickles	41.65%	34	Raoul Heertje	27.78%	55=	Spike Milligan	18.18%
	Moray Hunter	41.65%	35	Kelvin McKenzie	27.27%		Ken Livingstone	18.18%
15	Janet Street-Porter	40.00%	36=	Arthur Smith	26.10%	57	Glenda Jackson MP	15.38%
16	Ian Hislop	37.89%		Richard Coles	26.10%	58	Felix Dexter	14.28%
17	Alan Davies	37.88%	38=	Alex Salmond MP	25.00%	59	Mike Yarwood	12.50%
18	Andrew Morton	37.50%		Alan Coren	25.00%	60	Frank Skinner	11.11%
19	Rupert Allason MP	36.36%		Steve Wright	25.00%	61	Terry Christian	10.00%
20	Piers Morgan	35.70%		Neil Morrisey	25.00%	62=	Rich Hall	9.09%
21	Max Clifford	35.50%	42	PJ O'Rourke	24.99%		Andrew Neil	9.09%

CLUNES

MORRISEY

Top dog is Saudi dissident, Dr Muhammed Al-Masari, a professor of Islamic Law. What this says about the question-setting, God knows. As, indeed, does Allah. Of all the guests to be invited onto the show, Dr Al-Masari's appearance generated the most complaints, showing once again this country's sad habit of always wanting to knock a winner.

Many will be surprised that the editor of *Private Eye* came off second best to a seedy film director, the BBC's top sitcom star and a National Lottery Show presenter, and considerably less surprised that he came off second best to a judge.

MARTIN CLUNES and **NEIL MORRISEY**, stars of top-rating BBC1 sitcom **MEN BEHAVING BADLY** scored 21.59 per cent and 25 per cent respectively. Not especially interesting, but sufficient excuse for us to print large photos of these extremely popular and saleable comedy stars.

Terry Major-Ball's score of 22.22 per cent underlined what many will have suspected, that his understanding of current affairs is by far the highest in his family.

Max Clifford said he was delighted to have scored more than 50 per cent. And, incredibly, some people believed him.

At the bottom of the heap, the prize for bone-headed ignorance is shared by Rich Hall and Andrew Neil. Rich Hall's excuse is that he is an American. Andrew Neil, of course, used to be editor of *The Sunday Times*.

8 Saturday

9 Sunday

Anniversary – Shergar stolen (1983)
Although Shergar's remains have never been found, it is believed he was kidnapped by the IRA, who did away with him after he refused to talk.

Shergar is reckoned to be dead by everyone except the company that insured his life, Norwich Union. One of the horse's owners said 'Norwich Union has a moral obligation to pay. They're relying on small print to wriggle out of responsibility'. Difficult to believe of an insurance company.

10 Monday

11 Tuesday

Shrove Tuesday – Pancake Day
Or 'Black Tuesday', as it's known in certain fat product circles.

12 Wednesday

Thursday 13

Friday 14

Saint Valentine's Day

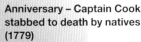

Anniversary – Captain Cook stabbed to death by natives (1779)

For not sending them a card

Saturday 15

Birthday – Clare Short MP (b.1946)

Clare Short has frequently clashed with the Labour Party hierarchy over her outspoken views, not least in her campaigning for the legalization of cannabis. Unlike Tony Blair, the President of the Cannabis Legal Reform Group has backed Ms Short, saying 'contrary to clinical studies, cannabis does not damage human lungs, impair memory or damage human lungs'.

Sunday 16

New government bike-parking scheme revealed.

Unemployed used for speed bumps.

Naked sky-diving tragedy.

Have you tried 'Head and Shoulders'?

Liam and Noel Gallagher chill out backstage.

Turned out nice again.

17 Monday

18 Tuesday

19 Wednesday

Birthday – Prince Andrew (b.1960)

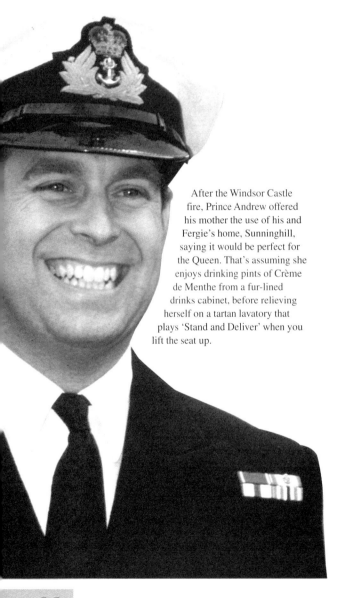

After the Windsor Castle fire, Prince Andrew offered his mother the use of his and Fergie's home, Sunninghill, saying it would be perfect for the Queen. That's assuming she enjoys drinking pints of Crème de Menthe from a fur-lined drinks cabinet, before relieving herself on a tartan lavatory that plays 'Stand and Deliver' when you lift the seat up.

Friday 21

Birthday – Madame Jeanne Calment (b.1875)
The oldest woman alive (at the time of going to press).

In February 1996, Madame Calment recorded a rap CD which sold thousands of copies in France. But then, that is a country where people still buy Johnny Halliday records. Still, her future as a pop star now looks secure as she was recently given a long-term, one-month record deal.

Saturday 22

Anniversary – F W Woolworth opened his first store in New York (1879)

From the humble beginnings of a 'nothing over fivecents' store, Frank Winfield Woolworth formed a retail outlet which became one of the world's most famous companies. The first customer walked through the doors in 1879 and, by 1881, had finally found the sellotape.

Sunday 23

20 Thursday

24 Monday

25 Tuesday

Birthday – Nick Leeson (b.1967)

Following the collapse of Barings Bank, Nick Leeson technically owes Barings the sum of £860 million. That's £859,999,980 lost in fraudulent dealings, and £20 for the letter telling him he was overdrawn.

26 Wednesday

Birthday – James Goldsmith (b.1933)

After James Goldsmith set up his own political party to push for a referendum on Europe, Jeffrey Archer entered the fray by suggesting that Goldsmith would be better off donating his several thousand pounds of campaign money to the Conservative Party treasurer. Although, as Jeffrey must have wondered himself, who in their right mind would hand over a couple of thousand quid to someone they hardly know for no good reason?

27 Thursday

FIRE CUPBOARDS ANGER DISABLED STAFF

It has been revealed that MOD staff in wheelchairs are to be put in cupboards when there's a fire. According to guidelines for new buildings published by the Ministry of Defence, 'there are to be cupboard-like areas where disabled persons will be placed for safe-keeping during a fire'. An MOD spokesman later admitted the choice of the word 'cupboard' was unfortunate. They've now changed it to 'oven'.

Friday 28

Birthday – Julia Carling (b.1965)

Julia Carling – famous ex-wife of the England rugby captain. Not so famous TV presenter. Princess Diana says despite her part in the break-up of the Carlings' marriage, that she will never write to Julia Carling to apologise – mainly because she can't spell 'apologise'.

Saturday 29

Leap Year Day – except in the UK, Ireland, Europe, the US, Australasia, South America, Asia, Africa, and Antarctica
Birthday – Gioacchino Rossini (b.1792)

The composer of many operas, including *The Barber of Seville* and *William Tell*, Rossini died at the age of 76, after a fantastic 19th birthday party.

Saturday 1

St David's Day
A day when, according to ancient tradition, every Welshman puts a daffodil or leek in his lapel.

Also starting today – Veggie Pledge Month
A vegetarian campaign to encourage people to give up eating meat and start nibbling at Welshmen's lapels.

Sunday 2

> Put not thine hand between the bark and the tree.

How WATER reaches your home

1 The sun's heat draws up water vapour from the sea...

2 The water vapour forms clouds of droplets which later fall as rain into Britain's waterways and reservoirs...

... preferably as far away from the British coastline as possible. According to the Marine Conservation Society, 'Bathing by many of Britain's beaches is like swimming in a public lavatory.' Except, of course, it's far easier to find toilet paper in the sea.

... unless you live, say, in the Yorkshire Water area, where somehow the rain seems to miss. The water companies continue to blame any shortages on the weather, even though they actually lose one third of all supplies – 900 million gallons of water per day – through leaking pipes.

3 Polluted water is purified in chemical treatment plants, making it fit for the population to drink from the tap...

4 If reservoir levels fall too low, the water authorities impose precautionary measures, such as hose pipe bans.

... so long as you don't mind changing sex. In 1995, Thames tap water was so full of oestrogenic pollutants that male fish in the river started developing female features. In a special study, those men who drank ordinary tap water were found to produce high-quality sperm; those who drank Thames tap water produced low-quality sperm; and those who drank Export Lager were sadly unable to take part in the experiment.

The best way to cope with a hose pipe ban, according to a leaflet issued by Severn Trent Water, is to cover your lawn with concrete. That's using a special mix of two parts cement to no parts water.

Severn Trent have complained that their advice to concrete over the nation's lawns was misrepresented by the media. So, to be fair it should be pointed out that they also recommended paving stones and gravel.

(and how money leaves it)

When drought threatens, the public are asked to take water rationing a stage further.

At a press conference, Yorkshire Water's chairman, Trevor Newton, said, 'It's quite possible to have a bath or a shower in half a bowlful of water' – although it was noticable that most of the press were standing some twenty yards away from him.

Mr Newton was later caught sneaking round to his mother's house – in a different water region – to enjoy a shower. So now at least it's only his character that stinks.

6

To protect the environment, raw sewage must be thoroughly treated before being pumped out into the sea.

As Minister for the Environment, John Gummer helped Yorkshire Water to sidestep the law and avoid the cost of cleaning sewage in the Humber River, by designating Hull as a seaside resort – even though Hull is thirty miles from the sea. At the time, one of Yorkshire Water's directors just happened to be a fellow Tory MP, Giles Shaw. One local suggested throwing them both in the Humber to experience 'the seaside' at first hand. Though frankly, a couple more turds floating down the river wouldn't make much difference.

7

Twice a year, every household in the country receives a water bill.

Most water authorities' bills have doubled since privatisation, enabling their profits to soar to over £2 billion. In fact, this is not a uniquely British phenomenon, as Northumbrian Water, North East Water, and Essex and Suffolk Water have all been bought by a French company. Lyonnaise des Eaux estimate that over here they can make ten times the profit that they are allowed to make out of their French customers, possibly because, in France, they're required to actually put some water in their reservoirs.

8

The water cycle is complete. Thanks to the process known as 'absorption', the sun's heat once more draws up water vapour from the sea...

The water scam is complete. Thanks to the process known as 'lining your own pockets', the directors of the water companies were allowed – just before privatisation – to help themselves to all the best investments from the staff pension funds. The result? A pensions shortfall of £450 million, which is now being refunded by the taxpayer. This would be an appalling scandal, if the nation's water companies weren't doing a superb job for their money. Which they're not. So it is.

Monday

Birthday – Brandon Lee [aka Brian McKinnon] (b.1963)

Brandon Lee, whose real name was Brian McKinnon, hit the headlines when it emerged that, at the age of 32, he had re-entered his old school as a pupil, and studied there for twelve months before being found out. In fact, he only gave his age away when he asked the teacher where the new textbooks were.

 ## Tuesday

Anniversary – First edition of *Today* newspaper (1986)

With its first edition, *Today* became the first ever national newspaper to print a colour photograph on its front page – the Queen in a flesh-coloured hat, offset beautifully by her bright green face and purple hair.

Wednesday

Birthday – The Reverend Canaan Banana (b.1936)

Reverend Banana, the former President of Zimbabwe, got so upset with people making jokes about his name that he actually passed a law banning them. At one point he had even contemplated suicide by slicing himself into pieces and jumping into a bowl of hot custard.

 ## Thursday

Anniversary – The Michelangelo Virus
Birthday – Michaelangelo (b.1475)

The Michelangelo Virus wipes out computer data on March 6th, the anniversary of the painter's birth. It's so damaging to computers that police officers have been called in to try and trace it's source – and, after several months of intense investigation, they have worked out how to move the cursor up and down.

 ## Friday

Saturday

International Women's Day

A day dedicated to women's rights on a global scale, marked in the *Guardian* with a special 8-page pull-out supplement, and in the *Sun* with a line-up of topless lovelies from all around the world.

Sunday

4th Sunday in Lent – Mothering Sunday

According to 17th century tradition, the day should be marked by presenting your mother with a trinket, a small sum of money, or a simnel cake (derived from the medieval Latin word simnellus for fine wheaten loaves) which can vary in form from the Shrewsbury simnel – a rich fruit cake in a glazed saffron bread crust – to the Bury simnel, saucer-like and stuffed with spiced currants, to the Devizes simnel, which tends to be star-shaped and crustless. Or perhaps just give her a card.

❝ Every bullet has its billet. ❞

10   Monday

Anniversary – First telephone message transmitted by Alexander Graham Bell (1876)

Alexander Graham Bell spoke down the phone to his assistant, Thomas Watson, with the words 'Come here, Watson, I want you' – which made Watson somewhat regret dialling an 0898 number.

11   Tuesday

Birthday – Rupert Murdoch (b.1931)

On his very first day in the world, much to his father's dismay, baby Rupert immediately monopolized his mother's breasts.

12   Wednesday

Birthday – David Mellor (b.1949)
Also National No Smoking Day
Unless you've just had sex with David Mellor, in which case you should take comfort wherever you can find it.

David Mellor is very angry about the way his words have been consistently misinterpreted by the media. He told *Have I Got News For You*, 'I am a pompous, sex-mad buffoon'. Or something like that, anyway – we can't remember his exact words.

Thursday   13

Friday   14

Birthday – Albert Einstein (b.1879)

Einstein is well-known to physics students everywhere, partly for his theory of relativity but mainly because he once featured in an episode of *Star Trek*. Aboard the *Enterprise*, Professor Stephen Hawking programmed the ship's computer to create a poker game between himself, Einstein and Sir Isaac Newton. In a very close contest, Einstein won, although Newton was down to his underpants.

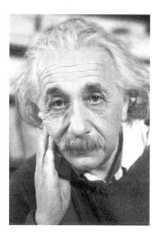

Saturday   15

Anniversary – Clothes rationing ends in Britain (1949)

Sunday   16

❝ Hang not all your bells on one horse. ❞

ODD | ONE | OUT

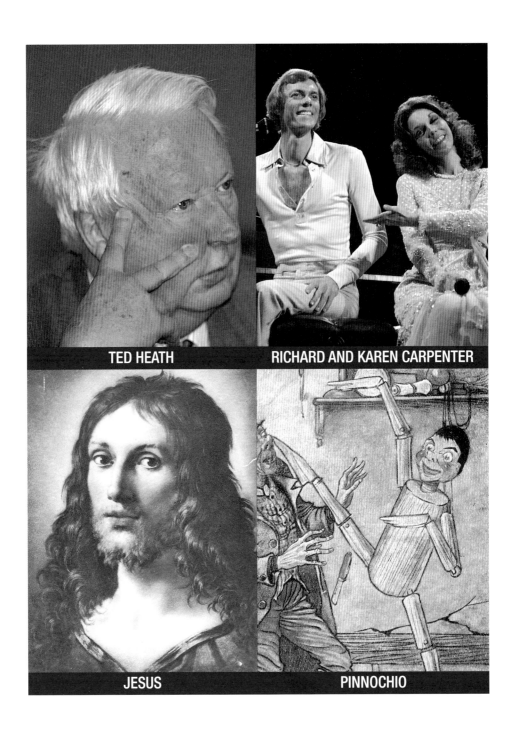

TED HEATH

RICHARD AND KAREN CARPENTER

JESUS

PINNOCHIO

ANSWERS

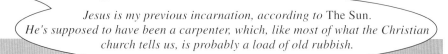

Jesus is my previous incarnation, according to The Sun.
He's supposed to have been a carpenter, which, like most of what the Christian church tells us, is probably a load of old rubbish.

Happy Christmas.

Not a particularly useful answer, bearing in mind that you two are currently seven points behind.

We need a miracle, David.

*T*he answer is that all of them were the children of carpenters, except for the Carpenters, whose father in fact worked in a car wash – owned, presumably, by Mrs Rose Royce.

*D*espite being the son of a carpenter, Edward Heath was recently awarded his own coat of arms. It features a green backing, representing his name, Heath; stairs, representing his birthplace, Broadstairs; and a shiny purple helmet... not sure which of his interests that represents.

*P*innochio's dad was a carpenter and made his son out of wood. The boy left home in disgrace, after Dad burst into his bedroom and caught him reading a fence catalogue and whittling.

*J*esus, the carpenter, of course, went into the family business, so we should be grateful that his father wasn't a builder – or all religious paintings would feature Our Lord with the top of his buttocks showing.

*There's a theological problem here, isn't there?
Because, strictly speaking, Joseph wasn't Jesus's father, was he?*

So you're saying that God wasn't a carpenter then?

Well, he did backing vocals on 'Calling Occupants of Interplanetary Craft'.

I suppose, if he was God, he could have knocked up a chair easy enough.

*Well, he did the universe in six days,
so I don't suppose a chair would have thrown him.*

Shall we pause for another hymn?

17 Monday

St Patrick's Day

18 Tuesday

Birthday – Judge James Pickles (b.1925)

Now retired from the circuit, Judge Pickles' first attempt at a novel, *Off the Record*, includes some breathtaking sex scenes.

'Yes, yes.' Ray's hand reached slowly towards the seat of rapture, the centre of life. He was drawn there as inevitably as eels are drawn to the Sargasso Sea, that calm area of the North Atlantic, between the West Indies and the Azores, where seaweed floats and eels wriggle their relentless way to paradise, as Ray was doing, or trying to do, towards his'

I didn't know you weren't a novelist.

I'm very proud of it.

Can I just say what a pleasure it is, sitting opposite a judge.

Thank you, Ian. It's very pleasant to be sitting opposite somebody who should be in the dock.

19 Wednesday

20 Thursday

Friday 21

Birthday – Michael Heseltine MP (b.1933)

When he took over at the Department of Trade and Industry, Michael Heseltine used about half-a-million pounds of taxpayers' money to refurbish his new offices. He also insisted that everyone at the DTI call him 'Mr. President', although oddly he rejected their pleas that he drive around Dallas in an open-top car.

Birthday – Brian Clough (b.1935)

The former Nottingham Forest manager, known to enjoy the occasional drink, was the victim of an appalling slur whilst doing the voiceover for a Shredded Wheat commercial. Allegedly.

When he hit that football supporter on the pitch a few years ago, somebody said it was a case of the shit hitting the fan.

22 Saturday

World Day for Water
Except in the Yorkshire area, obviously.

1930. The composer Stephen Sondheim was born on this day.

1948. Andrew Lloyd Webber was born on this day. Interestingly, not the first composer to do this.

Sunday 23

MISSING WORDS

Guest Publication – GOAT WORLD
(Australia's top goat magazine)

CALL ME ███████ SAYS FERGIE

 Call me if you've got a good idea for a book...

She's in an old nursery rhyme, isn't she? The Duchess of York, she had ten thousand men. And when they were up, they were up...

 And when they were down, they were down...

And when they were only half-way up, she was more than happy.

ANSWER: **Highness**

Wheezing Pavarotti Pulls Out Of ███████

 Goat.

Is it opera?

 Dame Kiri Te Kanawa.

We've just done the same joke with goat.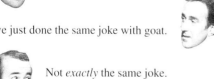

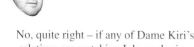 Not *exactly* the same joke.

No, quite right – if any of Dame Kiri's relatives are watching I do apologise.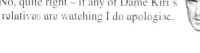

ANSWER: **Opera**

A TOUR THROUGH A GOAT'S WONDERFUL ███████

 CD collection?

World of Jazz?

 VE Day memories.

Oh yeah, 'The goats that won the war'.

'We'll eat again.'

'There'll be goat-shit over the white cliffs of Dover.' Or is it stomach?

 It is stomach. You obviously read *Goat World*.

Yes, just for the pin-ups.

ANSWER: **Stomach**

'All things considered, I think I'm against the cull.'

'Get me to the airport – and fast.'

'Spot the ball.'

24 Monday

Anniversary – 1877
For the only time in its history, the Oxford and Cambridge Boat Race ends in a dead heat.

Almost exciting.

25 Tuesday

Birthday – Stephen Dorrell (b.1952)

Back in the 70s, Stephen Dorrell lived in a house in London with Andrew Neil and David Mellor for several months, until eventually one day they noticed him. Looking back on those days, Stephen Dorrell says he remembers the time David Mellor announced he was off to start a family – it was generally around ten o'clock every Friday night.

26 Wednesday

27 Thursday

Birthday – Elton John (b.1947)

Elton John has his own, personalized coat of arms. The cryptic Spanish pun *El Tono Es Bueno* means 'The Tone is Good', the football represents his chairmanship of the Watford team, and the goat's hoof resting on it represents the quality of their first touch.

Friday 28

Saturday 29

Birthday –
Norman Tebbit (b.1931)

Anniversary – 1933.
Norman gets on his trike.

Sunday 30

Birthday – Piers Morgan (b.1965)

Editor of the *Daily Mirror* (or at least he was when he appeared on *Have I Got News For You*). Former editor of the *News of the World*.

Did you get sacked?

'Sacked', did you say? That's a very serious allegation.

Well, did you?

No, I didn't get sacked. But I'm glad you said it, because that's going to pay for my holiday. Thanks.

I can just imagine the jury finding for the editor of the News Of The World.

Almost like finding for the editor of Private Eye, isn't it?
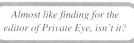

❛ When bail is highest, boot is nighest. ❜

31 Monday

Birthday – Alan Duncan MP (b.1957)

Conservative junior minister Alan Duncan was forced to resign over a property deal in which he bought two council houses at a heavily subsidised price. They are now worth £300,000. He said, 'There was nothing improper about my original purchase of these council houses – I bought them off Westminster Council.' That's like saying 'I didn't steal this money. I was given it by Ronald Biggs.' One of the houses is occupied by a frail 75-year-old pensioner, who has the right to stay there in perpetuity. 'If he lives to the ripe old age of 100, then I'll have a sitting tenant living in my house for the next 25 years,' said Duncan, as he let in the Gas Board to disconnect the central heating for the winter.

1 Tuesday

Anniversary – First Dr Marten boot patented (1960)

The Doc Marten boot was devised in the 1950s by Dr Klaus Maertens, who got the idea after kicking the shit out of Dr Scholl.

2 Wednesday

Anniversary – Argentinian invasion of the Falkland Islands (1982)
Starting point of the war Britain fought to prove that disputes shouldn't be settled by force.

Since the Falklands War, Port Stanley has been expanding rapidly, and enjoying an economic boom. Nowadays, the town even has a red light district – someone's tied a sheep to a lamppost.

Thursday 3

Birthday – Helmut Kohl (b.1930)

German Chancellor Helmut Kohl recently published a cookbook, which consisted of a culinary journey through all his favourite regions of Germany. Rather worryingly, it includes Polish sausage, Hungarian goulash, and stew from parts of the Sudetenland.

Friday 4

Saturday 5

Daylight Saving begins
– clocks go forward by one hour. Or is it back?

Sunday 6

Birthday – Max Clifford (b.1943)

Public relations consultant Max Clifford was once described by David Mellor as 'the sleazeball of all sleazeballs'. Though, coming from David Mellor, it was probably meant as a compliment.

So, did you make it all up, that stuff about David Mellor wearing a Chelsea strip in bed?

If you look like David Mellor, you've got to wear anything you can to distract from the face, haven't you?

❝ Draw not your bow till your arrow is fixed. ❞

7 Monday

World Health Day

> A device or arrangement that may be used to permit a patient to lie down, when the need to do so is a consequence of the patient's condition, rather than a need for active intervention, such as examination, diagnostic investigation, manipulative treatment, obstetric delivery, or transport.

This somewhat longwinded definition of a 'bed' was written for hospitals by the Committee for Regulating Information Requirement in the Value For Money Unit of the National Health Service (or 'admin', as they used to be called). In fact, the definition is already out of date. Nowadays, when people want to lie down in a hospital, they do so in a 'corridor' – or 'long interior alleyway connecting a number of rooms.'

Birthday – Cedric Brown (b.1935)
(former Chairman of British Gas)

Cedric Brown hit the headlines when he was awarded a £200,000 pay rise by British Gas, just a week after John Major specifically ordered industry chiefs to keep salaries down. Don't you just love being in control?

8 Tuesday

9 Wednesday

10 Thursday

The 100th day of the year.

Quite a milestone. But does anyone celebrate it?

No.

Admittedly, it's only a number, so to some extent it's totally meaningless, but then again, when you think about the fuss people are already making about the bloody Millenium...

Go on – have a pint.

Friday 11

Saturday 12

Sunday 13

Birthday – Alan Clark (b.1928)

Alan Clark lives in Saltwood Castle, but disapproves of most forms of hunting and lives almost entirely on vegetables. However, he's not strictly a vegetarian because he does have the occasional game bird. And their daughters as well.

After Clark had slept with the wife and daughters of Judge James Harkess, one of the girls, Josephine, described the ghastly ordeal.

'All I got were a few minutes of sex. I remember him leaving and I can remember feeling dirty. He made me feel like a dog. There was no tenderness, no love.'

'He came round the next night and I slept with him again.'

Obviously just to make sure it was as ghastly as she thought it had been.

Birthday – Gary Kasparov (b.1963)

When the World Chess Champion played against the computer 'Deep Blue', he lost the first game and was in trouble in the second – until he came up with one brilliant move. He leant across and pulled the plug out.

> Never put off till tomorrow what canst be done today.

British Airways – Complaints Procedure

as experienced by BA shareholder and Executive Club member, John Gorman.

John Gorman is a former Detective Constable, a hero of the Brighton bomb rescue, who inhaled so much brown asbestos digging people out of the Grand Hotel rubble that he was forced to retire on health grounds. In 1993, on a BA flight to New York, he made the mistake of asking for a brandy and coke.

British Airways is an airline. In 1993 they paid their business rival Richard Branson £600,000 in damages after admitting to a dirty tricks operation against Virgin Airlines. After an earlier dirty tricks operation, BA paid Sir Freddie Laker £10 million to call off legal proceedings against them.

---

1 THE MOMENT YOU EXPERIENCE ANY DISCOMFORT, PLEASE INFORM THE CABIN CREW

Whilst drinking his complimentary brandy and coke, John Gorman suddenly found himself swallowing broken glass. The crew apologised immediately.

2 YOUR CONCERNS WILL BE DEALT WITH PROMPTLY AND EFFICIENTLY

After receiving hospital treatment, Gorman requested compensation from BA for his medical expenses. Instead of paying up, BA denied the incident had ever happened, called him a 'Virgin Stooge' and told him, 'Go and fly with your friend Richard Branson.'

3 WE WILL BE DELIGHTED TO PAY YOU A HOME VISIT

Shortly after Gorman's claim was rejected, his home was raided by seven policemen and a British Airways official. He was arrested for 'conspiracy to defraud BA'. The police took away all the legal papers relating to his complaint.

4 THE PERSONAL TOUCH IS ALL

The conspiracy charges against Gorman were soon dropped, but he then received a phone call, traced to British Airways' security office, telling him, 'We'll get you next time, you arsehole.'

5 DAY OR NIGHT, YOU WILL HAVE OUR FULLEST ATTENTION

After several late-night calls, Gorman was warned, 'Any morning now, nice and early, we're coming to arrest you, smart arse. We think you're a raving poofter.'

He was going to report the incident to Heathrow Police Station, until the telephone call was traced... to Heathrow Police Station.

6 ALWAYS READY WITH A SOOTHING WORD

Some of Gorman's legal documents were eventually returned to him, together with a piece of BA headed notepaper, bearing the message, 'Happy holiday, arsehole.' Obviously the slogan that came a close second to 'The World's Favourite Airline'.

7 SHOULD YOU PREFER TO VISIT OUR PREMISES, OUR EXCELLENT PARKING FACILITIES ARE AT YOUR DISPOSAL

While Gorman was in a meeting with BA lawyers, discussing his claim, his car was broken into in Heathrow Car Park, and more legal documents were taken.

8 EVEN BETTER, WHY NOT RELAX WHILE WE PERFORM A ROUTINE SERVICE ON YOUR VEHICLE

While Gorman was in hospital for further surgery, his car was vandalised with spray paint. Police were baffled as to which organization could have done this. They examined flakes of paint and studied footprints, but still had no clue as to who could have sprayed 'NO WIN WITH BA' all over his car.

9 WE'LL TAKE MORE CARE OF YOU

Still pursuing his claim, John Gorman was beaten up in his home by two men who stole more documents, sprayed mace in his eyes and screamed, 'This is what you get when you mess with BA'. Suddenly Aeroflot seems like an attractive propostion.

10 OUR RECORD SPEAKS FOR ITSELF

The directors of British Airways claim they knew nothing about the dirty tricks campaigns against Freddie Laker and Richard Branson. BA was found guilty in both of those cases. Now they claim to know nothing about a dirty tricks campaign against John Gorman. Clearly, there's only one word for these sort of people.

BBC NEWS JUST IN

Salman Rushdie announces that, since the situation has eased in Tehran, he's now able to spend the odd Sunday afternoon relaxing in the park.

Welsh scientists perfect a sheep-detecting device, but admit they need to work on improving the range.

In Tokyo, the sumo-wrestling world is rocked by allegations of match-rigging.

There's further evidence that Tony Blair may be swinging the Labour Party too far to the right.

... and the makers of *Birds of a Feather* unveil the replacement to play the woman next door who can't get enough sex.

14 Monday

15 Tuesday

Wednesday **16**

Anniversary – Sinking of the Titanic (1912)
The second greatest disaster to befall humankind on this day.

Forty-two years ago this week, McDonald's was founded in Chicago, by Ray Kroc.
To celebrate, here's a reminder of what can be found in a McDonald's burger.

The back legs of a mouse

In 1992, Eric Schneider took a big bite out of the McRib he'd just bought, and discovered he was eating the rear end of a mouse. There's a difference at McDonald's, you won't enjoy.

E-Coli bacteria

A strain of E-Coli bacteria in a McDonald's restaurant was said by the Department of Health to be responsible for a major outbreak of food poisoning in Preston. McDonald's took immediate action, and renamed it 'the E-Coli McBacteria'.

Birthday – Jeffrey Archer (b.1940)

A Nematode worm

In 1989, McDonald's apologised to a customer who found a nematode worm in his 'filet-o-fish'. However, they insisted that the worm was perfectly harmless because it was dead. Possibly because it had eaten some E-Coli bacteria.

No raw sewage – probably

Happily, you won't find any raw sewage in a McDonald's burger, although it did once flood the kitchen of their Colchester branch. McDonald's staff eventually cleaned the sewage up without any food being contaminated, although it would have been a brave man who tried the chocolate milkshake that afternoon.

According to a recent biography, Jeffrey Archer was once stopped by store detectives as he left a Toronto store with three unpaid-for suits worth $540. Police entirely accepted his excuse that he had made an understandable mistake. And so do our lawyers.

In 1994, Archer made an instant profit on Anglia TV shares, ordered in a friend's name, at precisely the moment that his wife Mary had confidential knowledge that the share price was about to shoot up. Archer denied he had broken the law by using inside information and said it was pure coincidence. So either he's a lucky beneficiary of a million-to-one chance or he's a lying git.

> ❝ Tis a fool indeed who loseth his Oxford Dictionary of Proverbs the night before the publishing deadline. ❞

MISSING WORDS

Guest Publication – PIG WORLD

IT'S NO SURPRISE AS IAN ▮▮▮▮ AGAIN.

 Hislop loses.

 Ian wins Hunk Of The Year – again.

 No, it's actually about Ian McShane. 'It's no surprise as Ian acts up again'.

He'd have to act up, he's only little.

 Ian McShane? He looks really big in *Lovejoy*.

 Oh no, he's only about an inch taller than you, mate.

Never mind, Ian, pet. Have a jelly baby.

ANSWER: **Acts up**

GUARD YOUR HOME WITH ▮▮▮▮

 A pig?

 John Inman. He's big and tough, he can do it.

 It does actually contain the word 'man'.

Inflatable man – it's one of those fake men you put in the hallway and people think there's somebody there.

John Major Man. A blow-up PM.

 To put in the hallway?

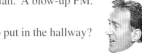

 Yeah. Does absolutely nothing. For days.

ANSWER: **A mantrap**

PORTILLO OWNS UP OVER ▮▮▮▮

 Gay love child.

 How can you have a gay love child?

 The love child could be gay.

 Owns up to the fact that he's got a face like a pig's arse?

No, it's actually about a trip to Amsterdam.

Really, if you just turned a pig's arse sideways, that would be him. Every time I see him I think 'what's that pig's arse doing there?'

 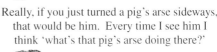 I'm sorry Paul, it's not from *Pig World*.

 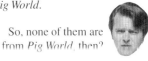 So, none of them are from *Pig World*, then?

 No, we just liked the cover.

ANSWER: **Trip to the tulips**

17 Thursday

18 Friday

Start of National Spring Clean
Find this diary under a pile of clothes. Think
seriously about chucking it away.

19 Saturday

Anniversary – The first 'Miss World' contest (1951)

The 'Miss World' Contest is still being produced in South Africa
although Eric Morley, the show's orginal creator, has fallen out with the
new regime because, according to a spokesman, 'Mr Morley felt himself
too much behind the scenes'. I think we understand what he meant.

20 Sunday

Birthday – Adolf Hitler (b.1889)

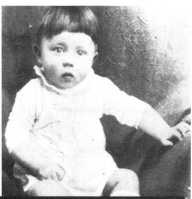

As an adult, Adolf Hitler (pictured here when he was 'Mummy's
Little Führer') avoided alcohol at all costs. Apparently he was
concerned that a few drinks might make him a bit aggressive.

Monday 21

Birthday – The Queen (b.1926)

Now that the Queen's geologists have struck gold at her Balmoral
estate in Scotland, Her Majesty stands to make a small fortune –
although she insists she's not going to let it change her way of life.

Also: RSPCA Week begins

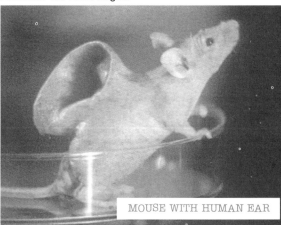

MOUSE WITH HUMAN EAR

'Pardon?'

Tuesday 22

> To say wise things is oft an easy task; to remember
> large numbers of them at eleven o'clock at night is
> nigh on bloody impossible.

23 Wednesday

St George's Day

Birthday – William Shakespeare (b.1564)

William Shakespeare actually shuffled off this mortal coil on his 52nd birthday, leaving Anne Hathaway heartbroken, as she had planned a surprise party. Shakespeare would, presumably, be turning in his grave if he knew about Quentin Tarantino's plans to make a film of *Macbeth* – 'When shall we three mother-fuckers meet again?'.

Birthday – Paula Yates (b.1960)

Paula Yates used to be famous for lying on a bed flirting with celebrities. After which she got up and went to work at the *Big Breakfast*. Amongst her many achievements, Paula has posed for *Penthouse* magazine, although she was careful to show only part of her breasts – the other parts were still at the factory.

Friday   25

ANZAC Day (Bank Holiday in Australia and New Zealand)

Do *their* diaries bother to tell them about all our bank holidays?

Birthday – Oliver Cromwell (b.1599)

Oliver Cromwell was once the MP for John Major's constituency, Huntingdon. Even today there are Cromwell Arms, Cromwell Inns and Cromwell Taverns all over the town, although interestingly no King's Heads.

24 Thursday

National Take Your Daughter to Work Day

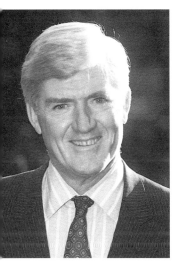

Lord Parkinson is highly unlikely to take his and Sara Keays' daughter to work, as he hasn't seen her since she was a baby. As the girl (13 this year) is currently the subject of a court injunction forbidding any public discussion of her, books and newspapers are obliged to refer to her as Child Z – though it's hard to imagine that even Cecil could have worked his way that far through the alphabet.

Saturday   26

Sunday   27

 A stitch in time saves no moss.

ODD ONE OUT

ROGET'S THESAURUS

A WHALE

IAN HISLOP

THE BRITISH RAIL TIMETABLE

ANSWERS

Is this about pulping? Because Private Eye *has occasionally, through extreme bad luck, had to withdraw and pulp the whole issue for mentioning various people. One was Cecil Parkinson. Another one was the chap I don't mention until the trial of his sons is over.*

So you can't even say Robert Maxwell? *You're not allowed to? Have you met that friend of mine, Maxwell Robert? Can you say Maxwell Robert?*

I can say there's a fat thing over there that looks as though it's drowning.

But you can't say Robert Maxwell, or Maxwell Robert, or any anagram of Robert Maxwell?

I think I'd rather not, actually.

It's funny because, years ago, I went to court and I can't say the word 'Bagpuss' – oh...

*T*he answer is that none of them have an appendix, except for the British Rail timetable. British Rail had to produce an appendix when their annual timetable was revealed to contain over a thousand inaccuracies. In fact, as you can see, the only accurate page was the front cover. Not a train in sight.

*A*lthough Roget's Thesaurus has no appendix, a new alternative version has appeared, including the phrases: 'politically correct', 'karaoke', 'AIDS', 'serial killer', 'paedophile' and 'ethnic cleansing'. They all appear in the section headed 'Brookside'.

*T*he whale, like all his whale chums, does not have an appendix because the appendix is chiefly designed for mammals that graze. Not surprisingly, the little-known 'grazing whale' died out rather early in evolutionary history.

*I*an Hislop was suffering from appendicitis during a recording of this pro- gramme in 1994. Immediately after the show, he was helped out of his clothes and given an intravenous injection of opiates. But then, you've got to wind down somehow, haven't you?

'No appendix' – it's such an obvious answer. What fools we've been!

Perfectly logical.

We should have worked it out, step by step. I'm sure that's what Robert Maxwell would have done. What do you think, Ian?

....

28 Monday

National Concrete Day (Germany)
Birthday – Saddam Hussein (b.1937)
Saddam Hussein's construction of the Supergun was somewhat delayed by Britain's Arms-to-Iraq scandal. Since the Scott Report, the British Government has only licensed the export of essential medical supplies to Iraq, including bandages, cotton wool and a 200-foot-long metal syringe.

Following the Gulf War, Saddam Hussein, dropped gas on the Kurds, and shortly afterwards Jeffrey Archer arrived to organise an appeal on their behalf. If only he could have got there earlier.

29 Tuesday

Birthday – John Major MP (b.1943)

The beef crisis, splits over Europe, the Scott Report and a challenge to his leadership… all these things came at a bad time for John Major – the 1990s. On hearing of the Prime Minister's resignation to allow the Tory leadership challenge, President Clinton released a statement which read, 'John Major is a great ally'. Although it was later revealed that a 'w' had gone missing somewhere in the text.

Wednesday 30

Anniversary – 1945. Hitler commits suicide in his bunker (made out of 100 per cent German concrete)

Hitler's bunker was rediscovered in 1990 by workmen setting up a Pink Floyd concert under the notorious stretch of no man's land that ran along the old Berlin Wall. It's ironic that such a discovery should be made beneath a place where people endured such misery and hardship – although apparently the support band weren't bad. Berliners have been debating whether neo-Nazis should be allowed to meet there, or whether it should just be blown up. Why not do both?

Thursday 1

Friday 2

❝ People shouldn't throw stones. ❞

'Woman licks chocolate off Malteser and finds man's head sticking out.'

'It's only a computer virus, you idiot.'

'It's OK, you only have to bow.'

BBC NEWS JUST IN

In Yeovil, the Liberal Democrats' policy advisers go out for a quick bike ride.

There are suspicions that the Duke of Edinburgh may have gone on a vegetarian diet.

The BBC expresses dismay at the opening title sequence for the Swedish version of *One Foot in the Grave*.

... and there's disaster for delegates at the UN, when the Reverend Ian Paisley tries his hand at simultaneous translation.

3 Saturday

4 Sunday

5 Monday

May Day Bank Holiday
The question of whether or not to keep the May Day Bank Holiday is in some dispute. Those in favour want it retained because it's the day when Morris dancing traditionally takes place. Those against want it abolished for exactly the same reason.

Also: National Smile Week begins
For God's sake, don't tell Tony Blair.

6 Tuesday

Birthday – Tony Blair MP (b.1953)

Tony Blair's attempts to reform the Labour Party have caused a deep rift between New Labour supporters and traditional socialists. The two extremes of the Labour Party have now come to be known as the 'Mods' and the 'Rockers', in much the same way as the two extremes of the Conservative Party are known as the 'Euro-rebels' and the 'Wets', and the two extremes of the Liberal Democrats are known as 'Simon' and 'Jeremy'.

INTERNATIONAL NO DIET DAY
An international day to combat 'the tyranny of thinness' that leads to the social oppression of fat people.

Go on, have a chip.

Wednesday 7

Anniversary – Publication of the New Register of MPs' Interests (1996)
In the new 'anti-sleaze' Register of Members' Interests, David Mellor admitted to links with several arms companies, Douglas Hurd registered his directorship at the NatWest Bank, and John Major declared his Saturday job at Mr Byrite.

> *It's an amazing argument these MPs put forward – that they have to have these extremely well-paid outside jobs or they'll have no connection with the real world. Funny how they don't get jobs as hospital porters.*

Thursday 8

Birthday – Norman Lamont (b.1942)

Ex-Chancellor of the Exchequer. In 1992, while Norman Lamont was pouring money into the ERM, the economy was in such dire straits that one house actually went on sale at less than the price of a Lada car. The catch was that it was gradually subsiding downhill – so, it was going slightly faster than a Lada as well.

When Lamont resigned, the first person he told was his mother, who curiously passed the news to her local paper. And so the story of the Chancellor of the Exchequer's shock resignation became a scoop for none other than the Grimsby *Evening Telegraph* – relegating the 'Man Found Asleep' exclusive to page two.

Friday 9

Europe Day
Does this include us?

❛ Whatever will be will be. ❜

3 Saturday

Fragrance Festival Week begins
Bob Geldof abroad.
Birthday – Liz Hurley (b.1965)

Occupation:
That Dress-
wearer
After the LA
police arrested
Hugh Grant for
paying for oral
sex on Sunset
Boulevard, Liz
Hurley told the
press, 'My dad's
initial reaction,
like any good
father, was that
Hugh should have been horsewhipped.' Not a bad idea, though it
would probably have cost an extra $50.

11 Sunday

12 Monday

The emergency services leap into action as Liz Hurley gets her toe
stuck in a bath tap and dials 999 for assistance.

13 Tuesday

14 Wednesday

Thursday   15

International Day of Families

David Mellor forced his family to pose for this ill-advised snap after
newspaper revelations of his affair with Antonia de Sancha. The
scandal became a major publicity battle between Mellor and his PR
man (Tim Bell) on one side, and Antonia and her PR man (Max
Clifford) on the other. And the winners were… Tim Bell and Max
Clifford, as they made a packet while the other two lost their jobs.

Friday   16

Saturday   17

World Telecommunication Day
Bob Hoskins buys another yacht.

Sunday   18

Birthday – Pope John Paul II (b.1920)
In 1995, the Pope made his own bid for the Christmas No 1 slot by
recording a single, funkily entitled 'The Rosary'. Those close to the
Pope say that pop success hasn't changed his lifestyle, although now
when he's on tour, he insists on having a crate of communion wine
and three nuns in his dressing room.

*I thought the Pope's record was
called 'I Left My Heart With Some
Franciscans'. He's just following on
from Pope Pius XVII who, several
years ago, released a rave from the
grave based on the Resurrection of
Jesus called 'Wake Me Up Before
You Go Go'.*

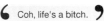

❛ Coh, life's a bitch. ❜

Paul Merton's Field Guide to Common Birds of the British Countryside

WOOD PIGEON
*Pigeon made of wood,
similar to clay.*

… AS RECORDED IN CONVERSATION WITH THE EDITOR
AT THE KING'S HEAD, CLAPHAM, TWO HOURS BEFORE
THE PUBLISHING DEADLINE.

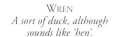

WREN
*A sort of duck, although
sounds like 'hen'.*

So how are you getting on with the field guide to common birds of the British countryside?

PAUL: Now prisons. I'll tell you all about prisons. People have been escaping from prisons before there were any prisons. Do you want the other half of that?

[PAUL INDICATES THE HALF PINT OF LAGER IN FRONT OF ME]

Not for me thank you.

PAUL: Well give it to me then.

[PAUL DRAINS MY GLASS]

PAUL: Thanks very much. Same again?

I only get an hour for lunch.

PAUL: You look at the Ancient Greeks. Though why we call them the Ancient Greeks when some of them were only thirty-five I've no idea. They didn't have any prisons because they hadn't invented concrete or iron bars, so what they did with the prisoners was they clamped them to wild horses. Not only were the prisoners secure, they also had regular if frightening exercise.

I believe there are several types of pigeon.

PAUL: Of course some prisoners escaped by sawing through the horse's neck with a hacksaw blade. Dry roasted peanuts?

BLACKBIRD
Actually not black or a bird.

I'm fine thank you.

PAUL: Quite often the Athens police would pick up the escapees after receiving reports that strange-looking men, stinking of horse meat, had been seen staggering down the High Street. And if you stand outside any kebab house on a Saturday night you'll see exactly the same thing today.

Isn't the woodpecker an indigenous bird in some parts of Norfolk?

PAUL: In the Middle Ages the Norwegians built their maximum security prisons out of soft scoop ice-cream. Of course the inmates tried to eat their way to freedom but not one of them ever managed to swallow E wing without being sick. They weren't too proud to try though.

ROBIN
Reliant.

MAGPIE
Shortened version of 'Magnificent Piebald', a sort of Spanish horse.

I will have a pint after all.

PAUL: Did you know that concrete and iron bars were invented simultaneously?

Lager will be fine.

PAUL: In 1787 George Bishop invented concrete and then the iron bar when he realized he had nothing to stir it with. That led to the birth of the modern prison and straight away convicts had to modify their escape methods. Sawing off a horse's neck and eating tons of ice-cream is no way to break out of Parkhurst. Which brings me to Parkhurst.

[PAUL PRODUCES A MAP OF PARKHURST FROM HIS COAT POCKET AND LAYS IT ON THE TABLE IN FRONT OF ME.]

PAUL: As you can see, it is a very detailed map – based on a satellite photograph, actually. Unlike most maps, this one tells you the precise location of Dogs Mess. It's the Governor you see. He hates the stuff, so the map is updated daily just so he knows where not to walk. He's a fair-minded man but he doesn't like excrement.

Are any of the prisoners allowed to keep birds? Such birds as you might find in a field guide to common...

PAUL: The Governor wouldn't have it. It's the droppings you see. You can't take a satellite photo everytime a budgie has a crap on a doilly can you?

Well I...

PAUL: Don't answer that, you might make a fool of yourself. Anyway I was talking about escape. With concrete and iron bars, you've got to have access to a metalwork shop. The first thing to make is a telescopic ladder. That's a ladder that makes faraway objects look nearer. Then, when nobody's looking, climb over the wall.

Supposing a guard sees you and shoots you in the shoulder?

PAUL: That's your second job in the metalwork shop – a suit of armour.

Isn't that a bit suspicious?

PAUL: Not if you wear it all the time. It's amazing what people get used to. You might get some funny loooks in

H.M. Prison Parkhurst

- Tailors
- Metalwork
- Church/Psychology
- Main Gate
- Football Pitch
- Dogs Mess
- White House
- Hospital
- Tennis Courts
- Gym
- B Wing

BLUE JAY
It's natural enemy is the trombone.

the showers – and if you do, you'd be more than glad you're wearing a suit of armour. The only thing you've got to worry about is a sodomite with a tin opener. Having another?

I must be going back. So, not much progress on the field guide to common birds of the British countryside?

PAUL: Well I had a look at it. As far as I can work out they've all got two wings and a beak, what more can I tell you?

So if I find some bird illustrations you'll do some captions will you?

PAUL: I suppose so, but all I know is this. Most birds are ducks or chickens. The rest isn't worth bothering about.

I'll see you around.

PAUL: Well you know where to find me.

DUCK
A sort of hen.

HEN
A sort of duck.

DUCKLING
Chinese duck.

1997

19 Monday

20 Tuesday

Birthday – Greg Dyke (b.1947)

On winning the television franchise for Channel 5, Greg Dyke told reporters, 'Running a television channel is the best fun in the world.' That must have come as a bit of a slap in the face for Mrs Dyke.

21 Wednesday

Birthday – Jeffrey Dahmer (b.1960)

Jeffrey Dahmer killed and ate seventeen young men in Milwaukee, keeping their bodies in a fridge. Controversial plans to sell the fridge at public auction immediately hit a problem – the little light doesn't always come on when you open the door.

22 Thursday

Birthday – George Best (b.1946)

On his 50th birthday in 1996, George Best pledged to give up drinking for a whole year. The next morning he woke up clutching his temples saying 'Christ, I hope I didn't say anything stupid last night'.

Friday 23

Saturday 24

Birthday – Stephen Norris MP (b.1945)

Transport minister Steven Norris, famous for keeping five mistresses on the go at once, used to play the guitar. Curiously, he went to school with Paul McCartney and George Harrison and so could have become a rock star, but unfortunately his lifestyle was too debauched.

Birthday – Eric Cantona (b.1966)

Following his infamous flying kick into the crowd during a match at Crystal Palace, Cantona was sentenced to community service, which was to be discharged by giving training sessions to youngsters. Before they began, he was instructed by officials to tell his charges, 'Play fair, it's not good to foul.' Or, as he translated into French, 'Attaquez tout le monde'.

Sunday 25

 Better late than never – oh no, I've done that one...

Monday 6

Birthday – Michael Portillo MP (b.1953)

As Defence Minister, Michael Portillo has spoken out against gays serving in the armed forces, saying it's important for soldiers to be able to trust their colleagues. Whether soldiers can trust Michael Portillo is, of course, an entirely different matter.

Tuesday 27

Birthday – Paul Gasgoigne (b.1967)

At the beginning of Gazza's spell playing in Italy, the whole Lazio team roared and applauded when he turned up on his first day with a couple of hilarious pendulous breasts and an absurd beer belly. That's until they realised they were real.

Wednesday 28

Thursday 29

IT'S A HARD JOB... BUT SOMEONE'S GOT TO DO IT

Westminster Council have carried out a remarkably enthusiastic undercover operation to shut down a suspect massage parlour, during which no fewer than eighteen council officials and policemen fearlessly subjected themselves to an erotic massage.

Council licensing director, David Chambers, said, 'We had to pay eighteen visits to make it stand up in court.' Mr Chambers is now available for pantomimes and private parties.

For the whole operation, Westminster Council spent over £5,000. Still, what else is there to do with the money, other than fritter it away on school books?

Friday 30

Saturday 31

Sunday 1

Event – World Naturist Day

As customers in a Hampstead delicatessen celebrate World Naturist Day, there's a disaster waiting to happen at the salami counter.

 An apple a day... er, means you have to buy a lot of apples.

2   Monday

3   Tuesday

CALL THE BUM SQUAD

Shortly before the VE-Day 50th anniversary celebrations, a soldier undergoing an initiation ceremony had a live hand-grenade inserted up his bottom. Suddenly, a gerbil seems like a sensible option.

Doctors joined forces with the bomb disposal unit to remove the grenade, giving a whole new meaning to the phrase 'Danger UXB' – Danger, unexploded bottom.

The soldier admitted that it was an embarrassing way to spend VE Day, having his buttocks parted by a grenade. Although it did give 'We'll meet again' an added resonance.

> *I heard that they tried to pull the grenade out, and the pin came out. And there was a certain amount of talk along the lines of 'Oh dear, shall we evacuate?'. As a matter of fact, the guy had already evacuated. And it happened in Germany.*

> *Quite right. Anywhere specific in Germany?*

> *Yeah. Up the arse.*

> *It was Munster. Apparently, such initiation ceremonies have been common practice since World War One. Which solves the mystery of how the German army came to invent the goose step.*

4   Wednesday

5   Thursday

Friday   6

Anniversary – First Eurovision TV link-up (1954)

In 1996, disaster struck for Ireland when they won the Eurovision Song Contest – together with the costly obligation to host the next competition – for the fourth time in five years.

Back in 1980, Johnny Logan brought victory to Ireland with the song 'What's Another Year?' – about 3 million quid, at the moment.

> *Wasn't the UK the only country to give no points to the Irish?*

> *That should bring Sinn Fein to the negotiating table.*

Saturday   7

Birthday – Prince (b.1958)

Prince was originally named after his father's dog. So, he got off lightly, compared to his sisters Fido and Spot.

Of course, Prince is now referred to as The Artist Formerly Known As Prince, ever since he changed his name to this symbol...

An idea he got from the Wandsworth one-way system.

Sunday   8

> ❛ Red sky at night, shepherd's delight – red sky at morning... Ariane rocket launch. ❜

CAPTION COMPETITION

Man with very large penis stands at back of the room.

And the bloke who's got the little blue book is saying 'There's no need for that Brian'.

And the bloke in the glasses is saying 'I could rest my beer on that.'

Tiny people threatened by Shredded Wheat slick.

The dog is saying, 'Bloody IRA – that was my kennel'.

Big Bad Wolf hits town.

ODD | ONE | OUT

PRINCESS DIANA

ARNOLD SCHWARZENEGGER

JEFFREY ARCHER

PAUL MERTON

ANSWERS

This question's about body-building. The Odd One Out is obvious – unless you count 'Body-building the Pavarotti Way'.

This is a bit difficult to take from a bald-headed short-arse.

Good to see that legendary repartee in action.

Diana's the only one to have a marriage with three people in it.

Her maths hasn't got any better, has it? Hewitt, Gilbey, Hoare, Charles, Camilla...

*T*he Odd One Out is Paul Merton, as all the others have taken up body-building in order to perfect their physique whereas Paul, of course, already has the perfect body.

*T*hanks to photos leaked to the *Daily Mirror*, everyone knows about Princess Di's body-building. At the gym, she used to lie on her back and push up a bar that was weighed down with three hundred kilos of camera equipment.

*A*t the age of twenty, Arnold Schwarzenegger was voted 'Mr Universe' – a title that was fiercely contested by Tragnor, from the planet Thweeb.

*J*effrey Archer got into Oxford University partly on the strength of a letter sent by his employers, Dover College, claiming that he was a 'Fellow of the International Federation of Physical Culture' at the University of California. This turned out to be not so much a degree course as a body-building course, advertised in *Titbits*.

*I*n fact, Jeffrey Archer even went on to launch his own body-building course which he called the 'Pal Malviro' system.

*T*hat was the one Paul joined before the photograph was taken.

That's not fair, I was very ill that day.

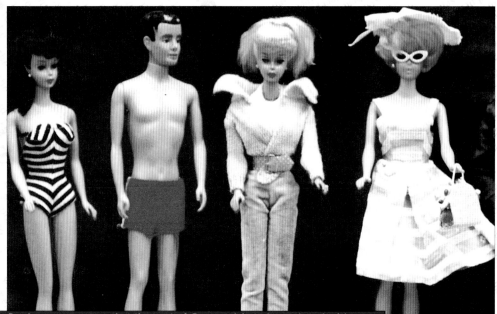

Producers announce that the cast of *Baywatch* is to be replaced with more naturalistic actors.

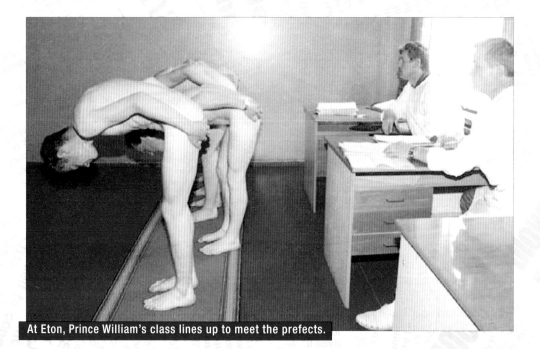

At Eton, Prince William's class lines up to meet the prefects.

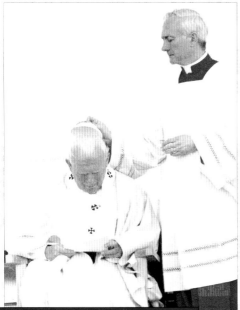

In Rome, the Pope is unimpressed, as one of his leading cardinals makes a ping-pong ball disappear.

On his way to the doctor's, Luciano Pavarotti is warned that he may have been a little overgenerous with his sample.

… and at a crowded London party, someone shouts 'Oi, Dickhead!' across the room.

9 Monday

Official Birthday – The Queen
(for unofficial but *real* birthday, see April 21st)

Various historical figures have died on their birthday – eg William Shakespeare (April 23rd) and King Lot Kapuaiwa Kamehameha the Fifth of Hawaii (11th December). It cannot be overstressed that Her Majesty the Queen, by having two birthdays a year, is in twice as much danger as anyone else

10 Tuesday

Birthday – Robert Maxwell (b.1923)
After the death of Robert Maxwell, his sons Kevin and Ian were summoned to appear before a special Parliamentary Committee, where they sat in total silence for two hours. Mind you, the question was: 'Name Alvin Stardust's follow-up to "My Coo-Ca-Choo" '.*

Birthday – Duke of Edinburgh (b.1921)

This year, for the Duke's 76th birthday, a giant imitation cake will open up on the lawns of Windsor Castle, releasing hundreds of snow-white doves into his line of fire.

11 Wednesday

12 Thursday

*(‘Jealous Mind’, for anyone sad enough to care.)

Friday 13

Oh-Oh.

Saturday 14

National Food Safety Week begins

‘You looking at me?’

Sunday 15

Father's Day
A special day when the man in the house is allowed, just for once, to put his feet up while Mum cooks and does the dishes.

Monday 16

Tuesday 17

National Day, Iceland

Wednesday 18

Birthday – Paul McCartney (b.1942)

Paul McCartney shares with the Queen Mother and Lord Lucan the distinction of having been mistakenly reported dead. Paul's demise was famously suggested by the cover of *Abbey Road*, although 'Mull of Kintyre' is rather better evidence of it.

Thursday 19

Friday 20

21 Saturday

Summer Solstice – The Longest Day

Too many cooks spoil the broth. Although, let's face it, broth was never that appetising in the first place.

MISSING SENTENCES

UNLIKE 'MISSING WORDS', THIS ROUND IS SET IN HER MAJESTY'S LAW COURTS
AND THE WORLD OF CUSTODIAL SENTENCING.

So, this is about people
going down, is it?

Master of the single entendre.

Don't you start on me.

No worries there, Julian.

I'll try and hide
my disappointment.

It would be a challenge,
though, wouldn't it?

I'd do it for charity.

Or you could do it on 'You Bet'.
In three minutes. You could have him
tied against the wall.

I'd have to be.

LIBEL VICTOR'S SETTLEMENT INCLUDES RIGHT TO ▮▮▮▮ JOURNALIST

Murder? Has that been introduced?

I'm not sure that would
work in your favour, Ian.

It's true, I've never won a case.

But you certainly know what
a libel victor looks like.

Big fat eyebrows, two sons –
oops! You can edit that, love.

'You can edit that, love' –
who's this now, Lionel Blair?

ANSWER: **To pelt custard pies at**

---

28 DAYS FOR JUROR WHO ▮▮▮▮

Juror who was watching the OJ trial
on his TV set? It's a great trial, the
OJ trial – he's obviously guilty.

He's obviously guilty? We haven't
had the verdict yet! You're an MP,
Diane – that's contempt!

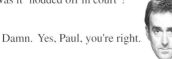
Was it 'nodded off in court'?

Damn. Yes, Paul, you're right.

ANSWER: **Nodded off in court**

---

28 DAYS FOR JUROR WHO ▮▮▮▮ ▮▮▮▮

Nodded off in court.

It's not quite that simple, Ian.

28 days for juror who invented
the concept of February?

ANSWER: **Swore at judge for
jailing him for 28 days**

Rupert Nobham seemed like any other Cabinet Minister – dull, untrustworthy, incompetent. But he had a terrible problem. He was…

ADDICTED TO SEX

READ ON…

At the Women's Institute...

Then, Rupert's boss held an important meeting…

Rupert sought professional help…

CONTINUED…

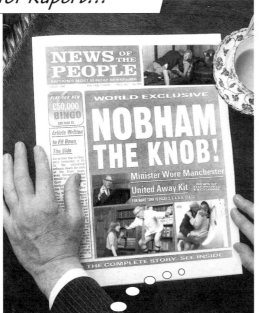

True Love Stories

THE END

22 Sunday

Birthday – Jimmy Somerville (b.1961)

23 Monday

National Day – Luxemburg
Anniversary – John Wayne Bobbit's penis is cut off by his wife (1994)

The film *John Wayne Bobbit – Uncut* includes a graphic reconstruction of the micro-surgery involved in stitching his penis back on, although more interesting for sharp-eyed viewers is the mystery blonde in the tiara standing behind the surgeon.

24 Tuesday

Anniversary – Jeffrey Archer wins £500,000 in libel damages from the *Daily Star*, over allegations that he slept with a prostitute, Monica Coghlan 1987

Wednesday 25

Thursday 26

Friday 27

National Take Your Dog to Work Day
Not much of an event for shepherds.

Far more of an event for shepherds is the regular 'Spot the Sheepdog' competition, run by the Westmoreland Gazette.

Instead of marking the centre of a football, you have to guess where the sheepdog's nose is. The answer, of course, is out of the picture – sniffing the bottom of another sheepdog.

A *Westmorland Gazette* READER COMPETITION

How close were you last week?

★ SPOT THE SHEEPDOG

One part of the case was that poor prostitute, who I felt very sorry for. And the judge kept eulogising about Archer's wife...

Justice Caulfield, you mean?

Yes, name the bugger, that's it. And this prostitute said that she remembered that Jeffrey Archer had a very pimply back. And that judge should have said to him, 'Take your bloody shirt off and turn round, let's see.' But no. There was an opportunity missed by that old creep.

 Fifty-two weeks hath a year, and for every one a fucking proverb. ❞

Saturday

Anniversary – Assassination of Archduke Franz Ferdinand. World War One begins (1914)

fact, a few minutes before Franz Ferdinand was shot, a bomb had
en thrown into his car. The Archduke promptly picked it up and
rled it into the road, where it exploded just in front of the car
hind. History's first ever case of road rage.

Sunday   29

Anniversary – Ladies Awareness Day (1996)

UNAWARE

Only one woman turned up for Ladies Awareness
Day at Newport, Isle of Wight, which featured
displays on health, diet and beauty.

(Daily Telegraph, June 30, 1996)

Monday   30

1997 – Hong Kong Reverts to Chinese Rule at Midnight
Chris Patten gets the hell out.

Tuesday   1

irthday – HRH, the Princess of Wales (b.1961)

efore her 35th birthday, speculation that
e might have just a touch of cellulite on
er body led to unflattering remarks in the
ress comparing the average woman's legs
nd Princess Diana's. And for once, there
as nothing between them.

The Sun said 'you've got a great lump on your thighs' and she said 'that's no way to talk about Will Carling.'

Cilla Black's got cellulite on her face. They've got to scrape her every time she goes on telly. Or is it Polyfilla? I can't remember.

According to an expert in The People – if such a thing exists – the best way for women like Diana to deal with cellulite is to 'eat less and take more exercise'. Perhaps not the best advice to give to a bulimic gym freak.

Did you know, if you have an affair with the wife of the heir to the throne, that's treason? It's 14th Century law – you can be put in the Tower of London.

The trouble is nowadays we'd have a pretty full Tower of London.

Wouldn't win the Triple Crown again, would we?

❝ He who doth the Shake and Vac therein doth put the freshness back. ❞

'*Watch out darling, there's a fork in the road.*'

'*Cancel the mini-cab, I'll make my own way home.*'

'*The monkey's saying, 'I told you it was cold, my bollocks have fallen off.'*'

2 Wednesday

Birthday – Kenneth Clarke MP (b.1940)
Birthday – Dr Brian Mawhinney MP (b.1940)

Kenneth Clarke says one of his proudest achievements as Chancellor of the Exchequer has been the substantial increase in the number of small businesses now operating. Unfortunately though, most of them used to be large ones.

As Conservative Party Chairman, Brian Mawhinney was attacked near the Commons by paint-wielding students who were protesting about the Government's asylum bill. After the attack, he said, 'The protesters know very little about this government if they think that we are likely to change our mind because of a few pots of paint.' Pots of cash, on the other hand...

In the security inquiry that followed, it emerged that Mawhinney's assistant, Alan Duncan MP, used his mobile phone to call 999 no fewer than four times, but the first three calls got mis-routed in the telephone system. A policeman did eventually turn up, but only after two deep-pan pizzas and a Strip-o-gram.

3 Thursday

4 Friday

Saturday   5

Sunday   6

OH WHAT A TANGLED WEB WE WEAVE

Research has been undertaken by NASA in Texas into the effects of various drugs on spiders and their ability to weave webs. The spider they put on Benzadrine, or 'speed', built its web quickly but carelessly; the spider on caffeine built its web erratically; and the spider on crack broke out of the tank, shot three researchers and robbed a liquor store in Pasadena.

The Spider on Marijuana.

The Spider on Benzedrine.

The Spider on Chloral Hydrate.

The Spider Formerly Known as Prince.

Monday   7

Birthday – Michael Howard MP (b.1941)

The son of a Romanian refugee, Michael Howard's original name was Michael Hecht. His father changed his son's name to make him more acceptable to this country – but sadly could do nothing about the face, the voice, and the personality.

Tuesday   8

 There be a difference at McDonald's you'll enjoyeth.

Hong Kong police express reservations about the design of their new riot shields.

There's a sensation at Royal Ascot as a flea is spotted on the Queen's hat.

The Aga Khan is not impressed, as his servants forget to fill his swimming pool.

Police have released the last ever photo of Dave Stubbins, who successfully tunnelled out of Wormwood Scrubs last month.

... and there's excellent news for the Guildford Women's Institute, as God agrees to open next Saturday's jumble sale.

⑨ Wednesday

Birthday – Paul Merton (1957)

If we had met a year ago and you had asked me to imagine my perfect birthday, I would have been hard pressed for an answer. I suppose I could have quoted the poet Shelley's response to the same question posed to him by the Gentle Ladies Quarterly in 1817.

'To be surrounded by loved ones as I wake.
To be surprised by gifts both useful and imaginative.
To bathe in the glow of the nowness.
To meet male friends in the public house,
Before going up west and blowing forty quid on a prostitute.'

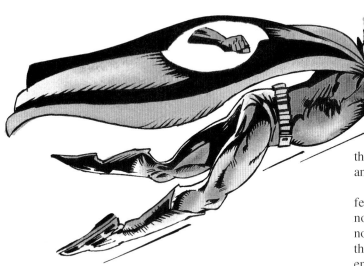

If you were to ask me now about my perfect birthday, I would immediately tell you the true story of my birthday just gone. I woke at six o'clock in the morning with a pixie standing at the end of my bed.

'Today is your birthday,' said the pixie, 'For one day only you are given the gifts of a superhero. Your job is to right wrongs wherever you may find them. Your name is Fists Titan and your costume is hanging up in the wardobe.' He then jumped out of the window and rode off on a motorbike.

I found the costume in the wardrobe and within five minutes I was in the costume. I then got out of the wardrobe, had my breakfast and flew down the High Street.

At the speed of light, I organised a petition to stop the local nursery school closing down. I gathered quite a few signatures and we should know the result in a couple of months.

Making my way towards the bank, I noticed the butcher standing by his shop doorway taking the piss out of my cape. I introduced myself as Fists Titan and told him that, whereas he was a purveyor of fresh meats, I was a purveyor of good deeds. I then wished him good day. With the word 'Tosspot' ringing in my ears, I crossed the road and entered the bank.

So far the opportunities for righting wrongs were few and far between. While queueing in the bank, I noticed that several female customers were wearing nothing but their underwear. At first I was startled, but then quickly realised that amongst my superhero talents must lie the gift of SUPER VISION.

By the gift of SUPER VISION, I don't mean to suggest that I had an uncanny skill for overseeing things. Far from it. Rather, my eyes could penetrate outer layers of clothing. As it was a sunny day, I abandoned the queue and made my way to the park, where I spent a very pleasant afternoon watching ladies walking around in their bras. Those five hours passed quickly.

On my way home I decided to test the outer limits of my superhuman endurance and discovered that after eight pints I could still walk.

I slept well that evening, happy in the knowledge that at least for one day I had helped to make the world a better and safer place to live in. I hung my beer-stained costume up in the wardrobe and dreamt sweet dreams of going up west and blowing forty quid on a prostitute.

Maybe next year.

10 Thursday

OH WE DO LIKE TO BE BENEATH SPAGHETTI JUNCTION

Birmingham Council have launched plans for what they hope will be Britain's newest tourist attraction – a man-made beach alongside the canal under Spaghetti Junction. An artist's impression of the completed canal-side development shows happy families sitting on deck chairs, pushing prams, riding bicycles and using anything else they happen to have pulled out of the canal.

11 Friday

Anniversary – Charles and Diana's Divorce Settlement (1996)

Diana successfully held out for a divorce settlement worth 17 million pounds. From now on, though, whenever she meets her own children, she has been told she should curtsey, and whenever she meets her ex-husband, she's been told she should duck.

Saturday 12

Orangeman's Day (Northern Ireland)
A historic day marking the enshrinement of every Irish Protestant's God-given right to sing, march and incite a riot.

Dr Brian Mawhinney – pictured here purely to represent a typical Ulster-born Protestant, and certainly *not* because it's quite entertaining to see another photo of him splashed with orange paint.

Anniversary 1962. The first television satellite, Telstar 1, is launched, a mission that ended in calamity – or Sky TV as it's now known

In 1994, the Queen Mother's death was accidentally declared, when a videotape editor saw a *Sky News* rehearsal of her obituary and rang his mother to let her know. Sky apologised for their amateurism and incompetence, and asked for the previous five years to be taken into consideration.

> Beelzebub has a devil put aside for me-ee, for me-eee, for meeeeee.

ODD | ONE | OUT

NIGEL SHORT

MARK LITTLE

GRO HARLEM BRUNDTLAND
(PRESIDENT OF NORWAY)

THE GRIM REAPER

ANSWERS

Is the woman at the bottom the only one who's been on a plane and the seat stuck to her back? And no one's had the nerve to tell her?

How about Nigel Short – 'short', Mark Little – 'little', and is Brundtland the Norwegian for 'tiny'?

I know! They've all been in Neighbours.

*The Grim Reaper was **not** in* Neighbours, *Ian.*

*T*he answer is that all of them have received death threats, except of course for the Grim Reaper, who just tidies up afterwards.

*T*he Grim Reaper is a skeletal figure, with a skull-like face and loose-hanging clothing. So, if he ever fancied a change of job, he could take over from Kate Moss.

*B*ig Breakfast star Mark Little received a death threat in the form of a telephone call, saying 'I hate you, I want to kill you'. The office secretary explained that that often happened if you picked up Keith Chegwin's phone.

*B*efore the Norwegian referendum on EC membership, Mrs Gro Harlem Brundtland received a bullet through the post. Fortunately, it was sent second class, or she could have been seriously injured.

*D*uring an international chess tournament, a Russian opponent's dad threatened to stab Nigel Short with a knife. Short spent eight hours considering all the options, then kneed him diagonally in the groin.

Why do people slag off Nigel Short? Second place isn't that bad, is it?

You should know.

Did you see the World Chess Championship on Channel Four? They had this thing called Predict-a-move, where you had to phone in and guess what Nigel Short's next move would be. And Kasparov won it every time.

13 Sunday

Birthday – Ian Hislop (b.1960)

Today is my birthday. This makes my star sign Cancer and since astrological systems assume that one shares characteristics with others born under the same sign, it follows that one must have a special affinity with those born on the very same day.

I myself was somewhat sceptical about the value of astrology but, after researching the identities of those who came into this world on July 13th, I can no longer deny its power.

Harrison Ford was born today. Not only do we look almost identical but we both have the same rugged charm and extraordinary effect on women. Incredible. Today is also the birthday of Mr Moss Evans, who was the General Secretary of the Transport and General Workers' Union between 1978 and 1985. I am not going to be 72 today and I have never been in charge of a large Trade Union, but otherwise we could almost be twins. Mr David Blatherwick, the British Ambassador to Egypt is 56 today. I have always wanted to go to Egypt and, even though it seems a bit dangerous for tourists at the moment, I probably will go there one day. Amazing. But the connections do not end there. Professor Ghillean Prance, the director of Kew Gardens is 60 today. And guess where I went for a walk last year? That's right. The very same gardens. Professor Sir Bernard Tomlinson, the pathologist and London Health reformer is 77. He is the man who suggested closing down Guys Hospital and I once had to take my son to Guys in an emergency. We share an uncanny joint concern with the fate of this marvellous hospital (even though he wants to close it and I think, like everyone else, that it should be kept open). What about Mr H A (Larry) Gomes who will be 44? He is a former cricketer who played for the West Indies. I myself play cricket on Wandsworth Common for a local side run

by Arthur Smith. And if there are any cynics left then let them consider this. Sir Richard Buxton, the High Court judge is 59 today. Why should he and I quite separately have thought of going into the legal business if not for reasons dictated by the stars and manifested in our shared birthday? As if that was not definite evidence in itself I have saved the most rare coincidence to last. What about Vice Admiral the Hon Sir Nicholas Hill Norton, the former deputy chief of defence staff who will be 58 today? Why did he join the Royal Naval College at Dartmouth when young, and I learn to sail a dinghy on holiday last year? Explain that without recourse to the movements of the heavenly bodies. And the list does not stop there. With every name that crops up, the only possible first thought is their bizarre similarity to myself. Try it. The Right Reverend Monsignor Alfred Gilbey, 96. Uncanny. The Knight of Glin, art historian, 60. Extraordinary. Madame Simone Veil the former French Government minister, 70. Unbelievable. Brigadier Dame Jean Rivett-Drake, the former director of the Womens Royal Army Corps, 88. Astounding. The designer Mr Lee Copperwheat who is only 31. Spooky.

I now firmly believe that it is all in the stars. Which is where the actor Patrick Stewart tends to be found whenever I see him in the series *Star Trek – the Next Generation*. And he is, would you believe it, 57 on July 13th. It all adds up.

Who in their right mind can claim that all these similar people are not bound to me by the same destiny? Happy Birthday fellow Cancerians and soul-mates, especially the 81-year-old Earl of Devon which just so happens to be my favourite county. Apart from Somerset. And Dorset.

I think astrology is owed an apology.

14   Monday

Bastille Day, France (st. 1789)

Bastille Day commemorates the occasion when a gang of French shop-keepers managed to break into the most heavily fortified prison in France, which was a blow for the security firm who had just taken over there, *Le Group Quatre*.

15   Tuesday

St Swithin's Day

A rare day of rejoicing for all men whose Mum and Dad named them Swithin.

16   Wednesday

Thursday   17

Birthday – Camilla Parker-Bowles (b.1946)

Former wife of Andrew Parker-Bowles. In January 1996, unexpected shame was brought upon the family name when their son Tom was arrested for possession of cannabis. During the police interview he admitted he was on dope, but then, at the time, his mother was on Charlie.

Friday   18

Birthday – Richard Branson (b.1950)

Branson is the man behind Virgin Records and Virgin Airlines. When he branched out into Virgin Cola, the *Daily Telegraph* wrote: 'He is seeking world domination.' A claim dismissed as 'nonsense' by Branson, from his undersea volcano in the Caribbean.

❝ Oh, this is hopeless. ❞

19 Saturday

20 Sunday
St Wilgefortis' Day

St Wilgefortis, a Christian martyr, prayed for facial hair to grow on her face, as a means of repulsing the unnatural advances of men – and has since been an inspiration to many a Bulgarian discus thrower.

21 Monday
Independence Day, Belgium

22 Tuesday
Birthday – Reverend William Spooner (b.1844)
The originator of the spoonerism. Born a shining wit.

23 Wednesday
Anniversary – Marriage of Prince Andrew and Sarah Ferguson (1986)

Divorced 1996. Royal watchers noticed cracks in the marriage at a relatively early stage – when Fergie failed to accompany Andrew on an official Commonwealth tour; when they went to church at Balmoral in separate carriages; and when she was photographed topless with her toe stuffed down the mouth of a bald Texan.

Thursday 24

Friday 25

Saturday 26

Sunday 27
Birthday – Paddy Ashdown MP (b.1941)

Many commentators believe that with Paddy Ashdown's leadership, the Libe Democrats would be where they are to In 1992, he confessed to having had a affair with his former personal assista Patricia Howard. She told inquisitive reporters, 'You have to learn when to your mouth shut.' And your teeth apar no doubt.

Do you remember that old joke about how do you get four Liberals on a bar stool? You turn it upside down.

No, I don't. How does it go?

I can't remember it, I'm hopeless at jokes.

❛ I'm finished in the proverb collating business. ❜

AN APOLOGY

On July 20th 1996 in the High Court, the BBC and Hat Trick Productions, the makers of the television programme *Have I Got News For You*, were each fined £10,000 for contempt of court in relation to remarks made on the programme by Mr Deayton concerning the Maxwell brothers. I would like to make it clear that I warned Mr Deayton about his remarks at the time and explained the legal situation to him on air in no uncertain terms. Not only was there a possibility of a financial penalty but there was a risk of a custodial sentence. In the event, the High Court were quite right to come to the judgement that they did and it is now only fitting that someone express suitable apologies. Therefore I am putting it on record. I am extremely sorry that the judges chose the option of a fine instead of putting Angus in prison for two years. I regret any distress that this may have caused to those viewers hoping not to see Angus for a few series.

IAN HISLOP

How to Fake a Photograph

'THE CAMERA NEVER LIES'. This unpalatable truth has long been a source of frustration to newspaper editors. It's all too easy to distort the truth in print, but what do you do when you've run out of words, you've still got half a page to fill and the pubs have just opened? What you need is a photograph. And fast. In the old days, if the picture didn't match the story, you were stuck. But not any more...

THIS PHOTOGRAPH of Labour's John Prescott out with his wife clearly shows him enjoying a bottle of lager. A tad inconvenient if, like the Conservative-supporting *Evening Standard*, you have set your heart on branding him a 'champagne socialist'.

HAPPILY THOUGH, Simon in Accounts has worked out how to use his computer mouse to wipe out unwelcome irritations such as beer bottles. Hey presto! *The Standard* can run their photo-caption as planned.

BEFORE

AFTER

Prescott: Champagne socialist.

WHEN HIS NEWSPAPER'S photo-fib was exposed, *Evening Standard* editor Max Hastings was forced to make a grovelling apology and pay substantial damages.

MAX HASTINGS has always loudly proclaimed his right-wing credentials. Formerly editor of the *Daily Telegraph*, he's a staunch Tory, who enjoys hunting and shooting, and spends a lot of time at his London club, which, appropriately enough, is called Pratt's. So, the last thing one would expect is to see him, back in the mid-80s, lending enthusiastic support to Arthur Scargill at a Socialist Workers Party rally.

Still, it's easy enough to fake, isn't it?

OF COURSE, it's not just journalists who tell porkies. It will come as a shock to absolutely nobody that a number of advertising executives have also tampered with the truth.

FOR A RECENT AD CAMPAIGN, the Ford Motor Company took a picture of several employees and featured it in posters all over Britain.

HOWEVER, when the photo was reproduced for a foreign brochure, it was deemed commercial good sense to replace all the black faces with white ones.

WHEN THE SWITCH was discovered, it resulted in a storm of protest and considerable embarrassment for Ford. As many critics pointed out, the picture should have reflected the true situation on the factory floor, and replaced both sets of workers with robots.

MPs, MORE THAN ANYONE, know the sort of damage certain photos can do to their image. At Westminster, there is already talk of legislation to curb photographic malpractice. And who would fight it? In the interests of fair play, the public will soon have to rely only on *genuine* photographs, such as these, to show politicians in their true and proper light.

28 Monday

National Day, Peru

Peruvian Television announces the launch of their new programme 'One Man and His Llama'.

29 Tuesday

Birthday – Benito Mussolini (b.1883)

Mussolini is reputed to have ordered all photographs of him to be taken only from below, looking upwards. Eventually Italian partisans obliged by stringing him up ten foot in the air from the roof of a petrol station.

Wednesday 30

Anniversary – England win the World Cup (1966)
Geoff Hurst hits a hat-trick, Jimmy Greaves hits the bottle.

Thursday 31

Friday 1

Anniversary – Introduction of the kilogram in France (1793)
The thin end of the wedge. Under ludicrous new European metric laws, a case against a burglar can now be thrown out of court if the prosecution refers to his height or weight in imperial measurements. However, the success rate in solving burglaries will remain unchanged – 'bugger all' being much the same in either system.

Landlords now have to remember that, although you may order a pint of lager, you may not order a pint of lager and lime, unless you order the lime separately. But if you subsequently pour the lime into the lager, you are breaking the law again. Try explaining that to a customer at last orders on a Saturday night, without having the glass forcibly inserted 12 centimetres up your bottom.

It is also illegal to serve up a pint of maggots, which has created all sorts of problems for the owners of late-night mobile kebab vans.

Saturday 2

Sunday 3

 I mean, no one reads this bit anyway.

4 Monday

Birthday – The Queen Mother (b.1900)

On the 50th anniversary of VE-Day, the Queen Mother was spotted wiping away a tear as Vera Lynn and Cliff Richard sang a string of old favourites outside Buckingham Palace. Apparently she was upset, because as she had specifically asked for *Gaye Bikers On Acid.*

5 Tuesday

6 Wednesday

Anniversary – Atom bomb dropped on Hiroshima (1945)

One lucky survivor heads for the safety of Nagasaki.

Thursday 7

Friday 8

Birthday – Chris Eubank (b.1966)

When Chris Eubank was caught travelling on a train without the correct ticket, police warned him that he didn't have to say anything, but anything he did say was likely to be pretentious twaddle.

Birthday – Nigel Mansell (b.1953)

Since becoming a special constable for Devon and Cornwall police, Nigel Mansell has gained a reputation as a stickler. He'll book anyone for speeding the minute they go fractionally over 200 miles per hour.

Saturday 9

Anniversary – Atom bomb dropped on Nagasaki (1945)
No one has apologised for this yet, although in 1995 the Japanese finally said sorry for *their* part in World War Two. This isn't good enough, according to human rights groups, who want another apology from the Japanese – this time for the invention of karaoke.

Sunday 10

❝ I can say what I want. ❞

Prince Charles admits that he may have overreacted to the joke about Camilla and the randy gorilla.

Bad news for Labour, as the man they hire to record Gordon Brown's tax plans turns out to have a maths O level.

There's evidence that, even for those within the church, the Easter break is losing its religious significance.

At London Zoo, the search for the missing Frisbee is called off.

… and the producers of *Gladiators* unveil their latest recruit – 'Wet Fart'.

11 Monday

National Condom Week begins

The condom gets its name from one Colonel Condom who discovered that the penis was afforded some protection when covered by sheep's gut, although how he made that discovery is a matter for unpleasant conjecture.

12 Tuesday

13 Wednesday

14 Thursday

Birthday – Gillian Taylforth (b.1955)

Gillian Taylforth and her lover Geoff Knights unsuccessfully sued *The Sun* in January 1994 over allegations that they had had oral sex in a Range Rover. During the court case, in order to show the jury how such an act would have been impossible, Knights and Taylforth reconstructed the scene in the car park. After which, two *Sun* journalists took part in a reconstruction to show how oral sex *would* have been possible – a selfless gesture from Richard Littlejohn and Garry Bushell.

Ms Taylforth's plans for the observance of National Condom Week are, at present, unknown.

Friday 15

Birthday – William Waldegrave (b.1946)

William Waldegrave was strongly criticized in the Scott Report for his role in the Arms-to-Iraq scandal, but somehow hung onto his job.

A fitting birthday for National Condom Week – a prick in a cover-up.

Birthday – Mark and Carol Thatcher (b.1953)

When his mother became a Baroness, Mark Thatcher became an Earl. Which means that if he were awarded the OBE, he'd become an Earlobe.

Saturday 16

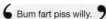 Bum fart piss willy.

17 Sunday

Birthday – John Humphreys (b.1943)

In 1996, when John Humphrys woke up in the middle of the night to find a burglar in his bedroom, he asked him what the bloody hell he was doing there. The burglar later complained to *Radio 4* about the aggressive style of questioning.

18 Monday

19 Tuesday

Birthday – Bill Clinton (b.1946)

President Clinton famously claimed that he once tried cannabis but didn't inhale, which is good news for his daughter Chelsea, as, if he'd been a drug addict, she could have been lumbered with a really embarrassing first name.

20 Wednesday

21 Thursday

Friday 22

Anniversary – All-day drinking introduced into British pubs (1988)

More recently, the Government has announced that 'Drinking Is Good For You' and raised the recommended drinking limits to 28 units a week for men and 21 for women. Drinking experts were divided on the decision to raise the levels. One said, 'Those at dangerous levels will just drink even more.' Another said, 'I love you, you're my best mate, you're great…' Health Secretary Stephen Dorrell said the main beneficiaries of increased drinking would be forty-year-olds and over. Presumably when they end up in bed with twenty-year-olds who are too pissed to know the difference.

Saturday 23

Sunday 24

St Bartholomew's Day

Saint Bartholomew's hospital in London was actually closed down by Henry VIII in the 1540s, but later he changed his mind because of 'all the myserable people lying in the street, offendyng every clene person passyng by the way'. Or at least that's how it was reported in the *Guardian*.

> See? Even the editor didn't read it, otherwise I would have been sacked.

25 Monday

Birthday – Sean Connery (b.1930)

Sean Connery was the first screen James Bond, although the part had already been played on the radio in the 1950s by none other than Bob Holness. Apparently, Bob greeted the news that Sean Connery had been cast in the film role with the words 'What 'C' has been given my job?'.

26 Tuesday

27 Wednesday

28 Thursday

29 Friday

Birthday – Michael Jackson (b.1958)

It's believed that Michael Jackson's marriage to Lisa Marie Presley fell apart when he told her he had always yearned for a little boy. Jacko has also given up performing in advertisements for Pepsi. Presumably he no longer fitted the company's image because he was turning from black to white, whereas Pepsi of course sends your teeth in the opposite direction. Allegedly, we've been asked to add. Jackson actually left the company in tears, after he asked what was in Pepsi and someone told him the main ingredient was 'Bubbles'.

Saturday 30

Birthday – Jonathan Aitken MP (b.1942)

Aitken had an affair with a prostitute called Paula Strudwick shortly after he married. At the time, Aitken claims he had no idea about his company's arms sales to Iraq, because although he attended the board meetings when they were discussed, he always left early. Well, at least we now know why.

> *Jonathan Aitken never made it to the Cabinet for years because he had a fling with Carol Thatcher and made her cry. And Mrs Thatcher thought 'Right, we're not having him in the Cabinet'. He was also selling arms, which competed with her son.*

Sunday 31

P.C. J.C. RULES OK

A new 'politically correct' Bible is to be published, softening all references to race, gender and the disabled. There will no longer be references to people being blind or crippled – which rather takes the edge off one or two miracles. 'Jesus waved his hand, and, lo...! The perfectly healthy man got up and walked'.

Some Christians now firmly believe that God has a female side. According to the World Council of Churches,' God has existed since the beginning of time, and is to be found in women.' Sounds more like Bill Wyman.

> ❛ I'm gay. There, I've said it. ❜

"'Reservoir full', say Yorkshire Water.'

'Wrong field, Mr Herriot.'

'A surprise photo opportunity, as Virginia Bottomley reveals her beaver.'

1 Monday

Birthday – Cecil Parkinson (b.1931)

Cecil Parkinson's job as Conservative Party Chairman came to an abrupt end in 1983, after the revelation of his affair with his secretary Sara Keays, who was expecting his child. Mrs Thatcher often impressed on Cecil the importance of Victorian values, but getting a servant pregnant and trying to keep it quiet probably weren't quite the ones she had in mind. After his resignation, some party bigwigs continued to talk about him in the context of a possible future Prime Minister. The context being 'there's no way this man's a possible future Prime Minister'.

2 Tuesday

Anniversary – The introduction of the Gregorian Calender (1752)
In 1752, Britain decided to catch up with the rest of Europe and change to the Gregorian calendar, which involved knocking eleven days out of early September – bad news for Virgos, good news for grouse.

3 Wednesday

Anniversary – England declares war on Germany (1939)
During the war, Josef Goebbels, the Nazi Minister of Propaganda, organized a broadcast to the people of Britain, telling them that Dover had just been destroyed by a huge maelstrom, when in fact nothing had happened. His senior adviser, Herr Michael Fisch, was sacked on the spot.

4 Thursday

1752. This day simply didn't happen

5 Friday

1752. Nor did this

6 Saturday

1752. Nor this one
Confused by the switch of calenders, mobs of farm–labourers took to the streets chanting 'Give us back our eleven days'. As a result, Britain's first Trades Union was formed, demanding an end to the nought-day week.

7 Sunday

Birthday – Queen Elizabeth I (b.1533)

Elizabeth I is reputed to have wiped her own urine over her face in an effort to alleviate the weeping smallpox sores that blistered there. Apart from that, she was one of the most charming dinner companions you could ever meet.

6 All this time living a lie. I'm gay and I'm proud. 9

8 Monday

Birthday – Harry Secombe (b.1921)

Believe it or not, Harry Secombe has published a diet book, under the title of...

Oh, don't tell me, it's probably called something like 'Goon For Lunch' – they always use punny sort of Goon things, don't they?

Yes. They've actually gone for 'The Harry Secombe Diet'. Incidentally, Harry Secombe's Highway was axed by ITV despite protests from ordinary families everywhere. They said this was the one time of the week that the family could all come together and throw things at the television.

PIGEONS HOME BY TUBE

A report in *New Scientist* magazine suggests that some pigeons have actually learned how to travel up and down the London Underground system inside tube trains – although some of them are, apparently, still having trouble with the Northern Line splitting into two at Kennington.

Tuesday   9

Birthday – Hugh Grant (b.1960)

Following the arrest of Hugh Grant and prostitute Divine Brown by the Los Angeles Police, on suspicion of having oral sex in a car, Divine released a record entitled 'What's Going On?', which were the words spoken by Hugh when the police turned up. On the 'B' side there's a track based on what Divine was saying at the time – which is an instrumental, presumably.

Wednesday   10

1752. Time travellers from another planet land in Britain

Thursday   11

1752. On a day that doesn't exist

Friday   12

1752. This is more than even time travellers from another planet can handle

Saturday   13

1752. Time travellers from another planet go home, give up travel, and content themselves with fishing

Sunday   14

1752. The Gregorian Calendar is officially introduced
Life in Britain goes on, in blissful ignorance of time travellers from another planet.

 Why did I marry Marjorie?

ODD | ONE | OUT

AGATHA CHRISTIE

MYSTIC MEG

ALASTAIR CAMPBELL

MELVYN BRAGG

ANSWERS

Mystic Meg comes up with predictions for the National Lottery – but not *the numbers.*

No, I think that would make it too easy for people.

Is Mystic Meg a novelist? Because she has written a novel.

What is it?

It's like a long book with loads of words, and you turn the page and there's another load of words, and it's all made up out of your own head.

*I*t's that all of them, except Agatha Christie, have written pornographic literature.

*M*elvyn Bragg won the *Literary Review*'s Bad Sex Prize. He was nominated twice, once for the following extract from his novel *Crystal Rooms*: 'She came to a climax, feasting on him, greedily kissing, tearing at him until the piercing moment when she shuddered on and he turned her, pushed in deep as she lay face down, fists clenching and unclenching as Mark drove in.' She then suddenly leaps out of bed, and shouts, 'Oh no, stop – we're missing the *South Bank Show*.'

*A*gatha Christie is the odd one out, as she never wrote any pornography. Apart from the scene where Miss Marple 'lay face down, fists clenching and unclenching as the Major drove in'.

*T*ony Blair's press secretary, Alastair Campbell, used to write pornography for *Forum* magazine, which featured the erotic adventures of a handsome young stud named Alastair Campbell. Although any similarity between this fictional character and any living person was purely egotistical.

*M*ystic Meg wrote steamy stories for *Men Only* magazine, although Mystic Meg is obviously a pseudonym. Her real name being Mystic Doris.

So, Melvyn, would you say your 'Bank manager bonking the 16- year-old' was pornographic?

We don't call it bonking in my novel.

Was it a bonk manager then?

Was it published in hardback?

Yes.

Some of those are quite difficult to hold up with one hand, aren't they?

15 Monday

Birthday – Prince Harry (b.1984)

After Prince Charles' TV interview with Jonathan Dimbleby when Charles admitted to committing adultery, the press reported that both William and Harry endured several days of torture at boarding school. So, at least *their* lives carried on as normal.

16 Tuesday

Anniversary – Black Wednesday (1992)

After the economic devastation of Black Wednesday, Chancellor of the Exchequer Norman Lamont famously proclaimed '*je ne regrette rien*' and revealed that he'd sat in the bath and sung 'Everything's going my way' – whereas, as it turned out, everything was going the way of the bath water.

The song *Je ne regrette rien* is, of course, most associated with Edith Piaf. Piaf became known as 'The Little Sparrow' because that's what her name means in French. Just as well the same thing hasn't happened to Norman Lamont, as his surname in French means something that would look rather silly beneath his grinning features.

'MATING SEASON OF DOMESTIC ANIMALS'

17 Wednesday

Thursday 18

NUMBER'S UP FOR COWPAT BINGO

The Swedish authorities are to outlaw the popular rural game of Cowpat Bingo, in which farmers bet on where the cows are going to defecate in a grid of numbered squares – a bit like *Celebrity Squares* and with roughly the same number of turds.

Friday 19

Anniversary – The Battle of Poitiers (1356)

The Hundred Years War between England and France is in fact reckoned to have lasted 116 years. The medieval historian who decided to arbitrarily alter the figures to make them sound better is now the patron saint of Employment Secretaries.

The Hundred Years War ended when the English hit upon a brilliant new way of occupying France. They would stop fighting, wait five hundred years, and then buy lots of converted farmhouses in the Dordogne.

Saturday 20

Sunday 21

22 Monday

Anniversary – 1995. Murmansk Nuclear Submarine Base has its power cut off. (Not a major historical event, but only just)

the far north of Russia, the Murmansk Nuclear Submarine Base d its electricity cut off after managing to run up a three million und bill. Unfortunately, nuclear submarines go into meltdown the inute the electricity is switched off, which meant the base mmander had to take over the local electricity board at gun point restore the power supply. A spokesman told the press that they'd een within a hisker of a rge nuclear plosion. en worse ill, he'd had spend ages -setting the ock on his dio alarm.

23 Tuesday

Anniversary – 1974
CEEFAX becomes available on the BBC for the verx f rs im . . jxcz nm.

24 Wednesday

25 Thursday

26 Friday

Birthday – T S Eliot (b.1888)

T S Eliot – close to Ian's heart for his poetic juxtaposition of twentieth century decay and mysticism in *The Wasteland*, and close to Paul's heart for being an anagram of 'toilets'.

Saturday   27

Anniversary – The first broadcast of *Have I Got News For You* (1990)

At the very first recording it was clear straight away that the show had some way to go before finding its proper shape, as Ian won.

Sunday   28

Anniversary – Pope John Paul I dies after only 33 days as pontiff (1978)

Do you remember when they had spent all that time electing the Pope and he lasted five weeks and died? I think it was the Express *that had the headline 'Pope Dies Again'. It's true.*

 I only married her to get into her father's diary publishing company.

THE WORLD'S PLEASURE SPOTS
AN ARMS DEALER'S GUIDE

Since the Cold War ended in 1989, the number of wars fought between nations has dropped to almost zero. But it's not all bad news. The 1990s have seen a drastic rise in internal ethnic and religious conflicts which, happily, can be far more drawn-out and bloody. Meanwhile, the Middle East and South-East Asia are still busy arming up for peace, so rest assured, your friendly local arms trader is still able to earn an honest crust.

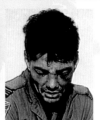

In the Register of MPs' Interests, David Mellor declared consultancies with several arms companies. However, the only financial reward he registered was for a TV chat show, to the tune of £5,000 – not quite enough to cover the cost of a brand new million-pound home in London's Docklands, plus a £300,000 house for his ex-wife. At the sharper end of the arms trade is RAF pilot John Peters, shot down during the Gulf War. Peters said, after his experiences, 'war isn't glamorous'. Unless, of course, you're the extraordinarily wealthy Mr Mellor.

✷ WAR ZONES OF THE 90S ✷
THE LONGER THE LIST, THE FATTER THE CHEQUES

1	Peru	26	Mozambique
2	Nicaragua	27	Somalia
3	Guatelmala	28	South Africa
4	El Salvador	29	Sudan
5	Colombia	30	Rwanda
6	Northern Ireland	31	Sierra Leone
7	Bosnia/	32	Uganda
	Herzogovinia	33	Nigeria
8	Croatia	34	Kenya
9	Azerbaijan	35	Algeria
10	Tajikistan	36	Afghanistan
11	Georgia	37	India
12	Chechnya	38	Pakistan
13	Russia	39	Bangladesh
14	Israel/	40	Sri Lanka
	Palestine	41	Burma
15	Lebanon	42	Cambodia
16	Turkey	43	Laos
17	Iran	44	Indonesia
18	Iraq	45	Philippines
19	Kuwait	46	
20	Yemen	47	
21	Angola	48	
22	Chad	49	
23	Ethiopia	50	
24	Liberia		
25	Morocco/		*For a bit of extra fun*
	Western Sahara		*at home, fill in the*
			blanks as they happen

When playwright Ken Saro was hanged by the military of Nigeria's General Abacha Major's government confirmed arms embargo had already announced two years previously would be rigorously enforced, soon as we had completed deli the 80 British tanks General needed to crush any democratic sition. Good to know that Brita has a role to play in international Even if it is as a mercenary para

When Nigeria's generals bu from Britain they take 70 per personal commission (anyone ever managed Arsenal will kn feeling). £1.68 billion of Nigeria ernment money – some stoler their own people, some received in kickbacks from W companies – is being kept safe by British banks for the General Abacha and his henchmen. A useful fact to your disposal next time your bank-manager takes the high-ground over your three pound overdraft.

President Clinton recently announced that the Americans want to put an end to violence in Northern Ireland. Well, they could stop paying for it for a start.

The Scott Report on British arms sales to Iraq contained the astonishing allegation that John Major and William Waldegrave may have 'misled people'. In the Commons debate, William Waldegrave was asked whether he had ever lied to the House and gave the answer 'no'. Leaving Labour no option but to call in a crack team of philosophers.

Saddam Hussein's arms purchases have been funded to the tune of £200 million by the British taxpayer. This is due to so-called Export Credit Guarantees, by which the British Government reimburses arms exporters when their customers fail to cough up. In total, £2 billion of tax-payers' money is gifted to the arms industry every year. With this support, Britain is now the fourth largest arms exporter in the world. So, even when it comes to killing people, we just miss out on the medals.

The £20 billion Al-Yamamah contract between the UK and Saudi Arabia was sealed by Mrs Thatcher in the mid-eighties. Mark Thatcher refuses to discuss whether he was paid anything for oiling the wheels between the Saudis and his mum, but it was such excellent news for British arms exports, who would begrudge him the odd 10 million quid for his efforts?

In November 1994, Douglas Hurd was carpeted in the High Court, after the Government spent millions of pounds of tax-payers' money – originally earmarked for the poor of the Third World – on subsidising arms deals. Mrs Thatcher promised financial help for the Pergau dam while she was negotiating an arms deal with Malaysia worth £1.3 billion. And, if you think you smell a rat, it's because Mark Thatcher was head of one of the companies that benefited.

29 Monday

30 Tuesday

Anniversary – James Dean dies in a car crash, aged 24 (1955)

In 1994, the family of James Dean threatened to sue the Conservative Party for using Dean's photo in a student recruitment poster. Wanting to attract youthful support for the Party, the Conservatives had hit upon the brilliant idea of using the picture of a film star who would now be the same age as Douglas Hurd.

1 Wednesday

2 Thursday

Birthday – Thomas Muster (b.1967)

One of the Duchess of York's recent lovers has been the Austrian, Thomas Muster, an unseeded tennis player. At least he was by the time she'd finished with him.

Friday 3

Anniversary – announcement of the verdict in the OJ Simpson trial – Guilty. (Not.) (1995)

Some months after his sensational acquittal, OJ Simpson came to Britain to be interviewed on the Richard and Judy show. According to the couple, 'OJ was the most controversial person we've ever interviewed.' The previous record-holder being Kenneth Kendall. As one of his many post-trial spin-offs, OJ launched his own drink, called 'Justice Juice'. It's the same as any other orange drink, apart from the opening instructions on the carton which say 'Cut here, then deny it'.

Saturday 4

Sunday 5

Birthday – Sir Bob Geldof (b.1954)

Former lead singer of the Boomtown Rats, Sir Bob will be remembered, of course, as the man who brought one of the world's greatest human catastrophes to the public's attention, by marrying her.

❝ And now I've blown it all. I'm finished. ❞

MISSING WORDS

International
CAR PARK DESIGN
& Construction Trends

Spring/Summer 1995

A PARKING Review PUBLICATION

Inside
- Structural safety
- Countering corrosion
- Expansion joints
- US airports plans

A practical update for architects, designers, planners, engineers and contractors

Guest Publication – INTERNATIONAL CAR PARK DESIGN

AA HQ INCLUDES ▓▓▓▓▓▓

 Statues of George Best and Oliver Reed. It's not actually *that* AA.

It's just word association with you, Piers, isn't it? Everyone else thought it was the motoring organization. Still, don't you worry, you'll get there. One day at a time.

 OK, smart-arse. Let's see if you do any better.

'Two vowels and two consonants' says Scrabble champion.

Not that funny, I'm afraid, Clive.

Well, I got the laugh by being rude about you, Piers, so it's all right.

Oh, they'll cut that out.

I wouldn't be too sure.

ANSWER: **760-space car park**

POLICE GRAB ▓▓▓▓ AT PALACE

 Car parking space?

Intruder?

 No, Ian, that's not it at all.

All right, I'm sorry. I just said 'intruder' – it could have happened.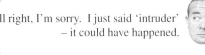

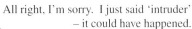 Yes, but it didn't. The correct answer is 'Police grab air pistol at Palace'.

Whose was it?

 An intruder's.

ANSWER: **Air pistol**

MERCY! IT'S THE ▓▓▓▓▓▓▓ NUNS

 Pay and Display.

No, the answer is Karate. The Roman Catholic Sisters of St Ann's Convent in Madras, India, are taking karate lessons. A fascinating story – which no one read, apparently.

Come on, Piers – surely you must have covered that story in the *Daily Mirror*.

What do you know about newspaper editing, Clive?

About as much as you do.

ANSWER: **Karate**

ODD | ONE | OUT

PAUL MCCARTNEY

POSTMAN PAT

PRINCE CHARLES' OAT BISCUITS

A PUBIC HAIR

ANSWERS

*That's the artist formerly known
as Prince down there, isn't it?*

*The Odd One Out is the pubic hair
because you'd be disgusted if you pulled back your bedclothes
and found any of the other three.*

That's not what I've got written on the card.

*OK, it's the Prince Charles biscuit
because you'd be embarrassed if you opened your mouth
and you had any of the other three stuck to your teeth.*

Nor is that...

*T*he answer is that they have all been banned in Japan, with the exception of Prince Charles' 'Duchy Original' biscuits, which are now on sale there. So, the Japanese sell us cars, music systems, videos and computers, and we sell them varieties of oven-baked oatcake. Who says British industry's on its knees?

A deal to market Postman Pat in Japan hit trouble because Pat only has four fingers, which, in Japan, symbolizes that he is a member of the Mafia. The Japanese were also a little anxious about the episode where Pat wakes up to find the head of his black and white cat at the bottom of his bed.

*U*ntil very recently, pictures involving pubic hair were banned in Japan. By law, any photographic model revealing pubic hair had to be touched up by the photographer. So, no change there, then.

*I*n case you're wondering, the pubic hair depicted in the photograph does in fact belong to the 'Queen of our Hearts', Princess Diana. And many thanks to Will Carling for sending it in.

*Did Diana call herself 'Queen of Hearts'
before or after watching that bypass operation?
Maybe for the next operation,
she'll be 'Queen of Kidneys'.*

*Or, if it's a vasectomy,
she'll be the 'Queen of Bollocks'.*

6 Monday

BIrthday – Melvyn Bragg (b.1939)

In his capacity as Head of Arts Programmes, Melvyn Bragg has made London Weekend Television's cultural output what it is today. One hour a week.

Birthday – Gerry Adams (b.1948)

Since Gerry Adams lost his Belfast seat in the 1992 election, part of his income has come from writing articles. In 1994 he came to London to launch a new book – apparently it landed in the back garden of 10 Downing Street.

This is journalism at its best, you know. For all the interviewing of Gerry Adams and presumably all the chat at the White House too, does anyone say, 'Gerry, did you actually ever kill anybody? Or do you just do the PR for it?'

Birthday – Bruce Grobbelaar (b.1957)

Grobbelaar's home was raided by police investigating an international soccer bribes scandal. They say they're now looking for a shadowy South-East Asian figure who is known only as 'The Short Man'. That narrows it down a bit. They're also looking for someone called 'The Blind Man', about whom all they know is that he's not blind. Which has rather cast doubt on the progress of the Short Man enquiry.

Tuesday 7

Wednesday 8

Birthday – Betty Boothroyd MP (b.1929)

In the 60s, Betty Boothroyd was asked by MI5 to keep a watchful eye on a number of suspiciously left-wing Labour MPs – a practice which has since been abandoned by MI5 and taken up by the Labour Party.

Thursday 9

Birthday – John Lennon (b.1940)

John Lennon's singing career continued from beyond the grave in 1995, with the exciting release of several Beatles recordings that weren't good enough to be released the first time round. This was after Paul's bank balance slipped below the perilous one hundred million mark – clearly Linda's sausages not doing quite as well as hoped.

The single 'Free As A Bird' required the three surviving Beatles to accompany an old demo-tape of John singing solo. On the tape, John had left them all they needed put a record together – three minutes of him singing and ten hours of him arguing with Paul.

Friday 10

6 I'll have to give the Mondeo back. 9

11 Saturday

12 Sunday

Birthday – Luciano Pavarotti (b.1935)

In spring 1996, Luciano Pavarotti was the subject of much gossip, after leaving his wife of thirty-five years. She was said to be crushed.

Birthday – Carlos the Jackal (b.1949)

Carlos the Jackal's reputation is so terrible that he has been linked with a number of atrocities which he had absolutely nothing to do with, including the Black September attack on the 1972 Munich Olympics the murder of the Italian Prime Minister, and the design of Milton Keynes.

Monday 13

Birthday – Margaret Thatcher (b.1925)
After her enforced surrender of the premiership in 1990, Margaret Thatcher was described in *The Times* as 'a figure who has dominated her age like no other Prime Minister'. She is the only post-war leader to have lent her name to an 'ism'.
Egotism?

At the crucial time when Mrs Thatcher needed support for her doomed leadership campaign, John Major conveniently disappeared to the dentist's to have some teeth taken out. Before she could kick them out, presumably.

Tuesday 14

Wednesday 15

Birthday – Sarah Ferguson, Duchess of York (b.1959)

During her career as a member of the Royal Family, the Duchess of York commissioned her own coat of arms.

Fergie said she chose the bee because, 'they're the epitome of hard work'. Of course, they're also round, poisonous, and airborne throughout the summer months.

❛ I'm going to run away with Ralph. ❜

16 Thursday

17 Friday

18 Saturday

DUMPED ON FROM A HEIGHT

An Essex family are the latest victims of 'Blue Ice', the slightly unnerving phenomenon of human sewage that leaks out of aircraft lavatory pipes and falls in large frozen blocks to the ground. The waste matter smashed through the roof of Mr and Mrs Palmer's house in Doddinghurst and ended up in a bedroom used by their student son – where it remained unnoticed for two terms.

Experts who examined the small, square, foul-smelling lump said they were amazed at how little it had changed since being served on the airline for lunch. A spokesman for the Civil Aviation Authority said, 'Out of three and a half million flights this only happens about twelve times a year.' Which will be a great comfort to the first person to be crushed to death by a half-ton lump of frozen shit.

19 Sunday

20 Monday

21 Tuesday

Anniversary – Battle of Trafalgar (1805)
not a BANK HOLIDAY

The campaign to have a bank holiday named after Nelson's victory at Trafalgar has met with considerable resistance. 'We've shelved plans for Traflagar Day because it would be insensitive and might offend the French,' said a Whitehall official, as he boarded the train for Paris at Waterloo Station.

Wednesday **22**

Anniversary – The Big Bang (4,500,000,000 BC)
Earth created. Obviously, there is some disagreement amongst academics as to the precise date.

Thursday **23**

Alternative date of Big Bang anniversary

Friday **24**

Anniversary – Maiden journey of Eurostar, through the Channel Tunnel (1995)
On the second day of the service, a Eurostar train carrying 400 journalists broke down before it had even reached the end of the platform – by which time the bar had already been drunk dry.

I think the trains are reluctant to go to France and I share that view myself.

Well, that certainly overturns any stereotypes we may have about judges.

We don't like the French and the French don't like us. I mean, they know all that. We've beaten them at everything in the past and they've never forgiven us.

I think they're better at speaking French than we are.

Saturday **25**

Sunday **26**

'*Freeman, Hardy and Willis meet up after several years.*'

'   '
......

'*Hugh Grunt.*'

27 Monday

Birthday – Glen Hoddle (b.1957)

A devout Christian, Glen Hoddle said that he wouldn't be making many changes to the team once he took over the England job, although the players will be expected to train in Aran sweaters and sandals. When asked about his views, Hoddle said that he had chosen Jesus. Once again, Matt Le Tissier cruelly overlooked.

Anniversary – First screening of *Blue Peter* (1958)

When the first Petra died, it was decided to spare young viewers any unhappiness and simply replace her with a lookalike. *Blue Peter* kept it a very close secret but there were in fact two Petras, three Sheps and, even less well-known, seven Peter Purves's.

28 Tuesday

29 Wednesday

30 Thursday

Friday 31

Saturday 1

Anniversary – Geoffrey Howe resigns from Margaret Thatcher's cabinet (1990)

Three weeks after Howe's bitter resignation speech, Mrs Thatcher was out of office. As a Cabinet Minister, Howe had a huge appetite for work and lived on just four hours sleep a night, which goes some way to explaining how awake he looked during the day.

Anniversary – Channel 4 begins transmission (1982)

CHANNEL FOUR TELEVISION

The very first programme to be broadcast on Channel 4 was *Countdown*, hosted by Richard Whiteley. Perhaps his other most famous achievement is that he was once bitten on live TV by a ferret. Whiteley himself has so far managed to resist the desire to bite anybody – quite impressive, considering that he used to work five days a week with Gyles Brandreth.

Sunday 2

 No more meeting Ralph for lunch at the Upper Crust Tea Rooms.

3 Monday

National Libraries Week begins
Mon – Thurs: 10am – 1pm
Fri, Sat, Sun: Closed

4 Tuesday

5 Wednesday

6 Thursday

Anniversary – (1991)
Salman Rushdie spends his 1,000th day in hiding

Before becoming an author, Salman Rushdie worked as an advertising copywriter, where he wrote the Aero chocolate slogans 'Delectabubble' and 'Incredibubble'. And of course now he's in serious troublebubble.

Anniversary – death of Robert Maxwell (1991)

Robert Maxwell was buried at the very top of the Mount of Olives in order to make his journey to heaven shorter. Little did he know, he was actually making his journey slightly longer.

Friday 7

Anniversary – 1993
The *Sunday Mirror* publishes secretly taken photographs of Princess Diana working out in the gym.

> *This was humbug week, it was absolutely wonderful. The* Sunday Mirror *printed these pictures, then the rest of Fleet Street said 'This is absolutely disgusting', largely because they didn't get the photos. I haven't seen them, though – not going to buy the* Mirror, *obviously.*

No, why should you? They don't buy Private Eye.

Saturday 8

Birthday – Rupert Allason MP (b.1951)

A maverick Tory MP who, when he's writing spy novels is called Nigel West and when he's voting against his own government is called something quite unprintable. Indeed, given Mr. Allason's fondness for pursuing libel actions, there are also excellent legal reasons for not referring to him as a conniving little shit.

Sunday 9

 We can get that little bar in Portugal that we always dreamed about.

BBC NEWS JUST IN

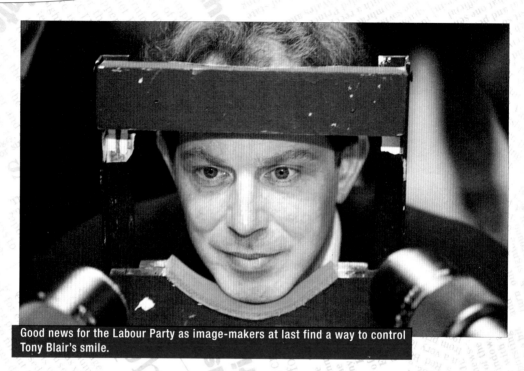

Good news for the Labour Party as image-makers at last find a way to control Tony Blair's smile.

Carol Thatcher puts on a brave face as a small drop of earwax lands on her favourite ring.

There are suspicions that an imposter may have sneaked into this year's Annual General Meeting of the Invisible Society.

There are still no winners in this week's *Puzzler* magazine's Spot the Difference competition.

... and before taking a short vacation in Los Angeles, John Major seeks advice on his itinerary.

10 Monday

Birthday – Sir Tim Rice (b.1944)

A much-loved, brilliantly talented, handsome and youthful songwriter, who wrote the words to *Evita*, *Chess* and this diary entry.

11 Tuesday

Veterans' Day

12 Wednesday

13 Thursday

Birthday – Earl of Sandwich (b.1718)

The Earl of Sandwich invented the sandwich as a tasty snack to keep him going whilst he was playing cards with his friends, Lord Hoolahoop and the Duke of Twiglet.

14 Friday

Birthday – Prince Charles (b.1948)

In 1995, Princess Diana deliberately timed the announcement of her *Panorama* interview to coincide with Prince Charles' birthday.

'Happy Birthday! I'm going to shaft you live on TV' – that's a nice present!

It's a hell of a present! And I thought they weren't getting on . . .

15 Saturday

16 Sunday

Right – I'm going to do it. 'Seize the day'. 'Be true unto thineself'.

17 Monday

Anniversary – The closure of the *Today* newspaper (1995)

The paper had previously been put up for sale in 1987, when it had to choose between two bidders, Rupert Murdoch and Robert Maxwell – in other words between the Devil and the deep blue sea.

18 Tuesday

19 Wednesday

Anniversary – Lincoln delivers the legendary Gettysburg address, at the Gettysburg military cemetery, Pennsylvania (1863)

Henry Fonda and Norman Schwarzkopf have both made recordings of the Gettysburg Address, as has Margaret Thatcher, who performed it on EMI with a lavish orchestral accompaniment. Lincoln, on the other hand, was overlooked by all the major record labels.

Thursday 20

Anniversary – Princess Diana is interviewed on *Panorama* (1995)

There is a theory that Diana times her most dramatic acts to coincide with important dates on the calendar. She announced the Panorama interview on Charles' birthday, the programme was actually broadcast on the Queen's wedding anniversary, and, if the reports are true, when Di pulled James Hewitt's trousers down she thought it was Christmas. As soon as the programme was over, there was a tremendous surge of energy on the national grid – apparently Buckingham Palace were doing a test run on the new electric chair.

Friday 21

Saturday 22

Birthday – Thomas Cook (b.1808)
Victorian teetotaller Thomas Cook invented the so-called 'package tour' as a way of distracting young men from alcohol abuse. Possibly the worst idea anyone has ever had.

Anniversary – Assassination of JFK (1963)

'You know what, I think my headache's gone.'

 I'm going to fax this off now, then there's no turning back.

23   Sunday

Anniversary – First broadcast of *Dr Who* (1963)

It goes without saying that Dr Who can't be a genuine doctor, as he changes into a different person every couple of years – as opposed to your local GP, who changes every couple of weeks.

24   Monday

25   Tuesday

26   Wednesday

Birthday – John Gummer (b.1939)

John Gummer is best known for demonstrating the safety of British Beef by feeding it to his daughter Cordelia – or Napoleon, as she's now known on the ward.

Mr Gummer is the one minister that John Major can trust not to have an affair, because if a woman's that desperate then she's already shagging David Mellor.

Thursday   27

Thanksgiving Day

Friday   28

Saturday   29

Sunday   30

St Andrew's Day
Birthday – Sir Winston Churchill (b.1874)

I was a great admirer of Churchill. I saw him speaking in the House.

He was an alcoholic, wasn't he?

Yes, pissed as a newt.

His state papers, which should have been given free to the nation by his rather greedy family, have been sold off for a fortune. The National Lottery, instead of giving 12 million quid to researching into cancer or saving small children who are dying, said 'Oh, let's give Winston Churchill Junior and his family twelve million quid.' Strikes me as rather revolting. Their grandfather would have had a fit.

No, he would have had a drink.

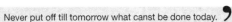
❝ Never put off till tomorrow what canst be done today. **❞**

MISSING WORDS

Guest Publication –
THE OBSERVER,
from the week
of VE Day 1945

HIMMLER'S DISGUISE
– ▮▮▮▮▮▮▮▮▮

As Eva Braun,
a bit of a shock for Hitler.

Queen Mother confesses – 'It was me'.

Fools *Blind Date* audience.
He was Number 2, he got picked,
went for a week in Benidorm.

ANSWER: **Black patch and shaved moustache**

U-BOAT CREW DID NOT KNOW ▮▮▮▮

Did not know they were in a U-boat.

The war was over.

Didn't know the answer – so you gave
the points to Paul Merton again.

Actually, I am going to give the
points to Paul Merton again,
because he got the right answer.

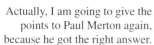

From 1945! That is sad.

It's important to read *all* the papers, Ian.

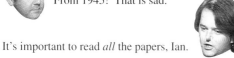

ANSWER: **That the war was over**

The World Will Be a Cleaner Place When ▮▮▮▮▮ Are Made Again.

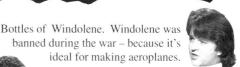

Bottles of Windolene. Windolene was
banned during the war – because it's
ideal for making aeroplanes.

I'm not sure that's strictly true.

It was vital to the war effort.
'Don't clean your windows, missus,
that could be a Hurricane bomber.'

It could be, except the Hurricane was
a fighter, not a bomber. Sorry, Paul.

What? As if they really *were*
making planes out of Windolene!
I do beg your pardon!

The answer is
'Goblin Cleaners'.

Is that a specific job?

ANSWER: **Goblin cleaners**

1 Monday

World AIDS Day

To mark World AIDS Day in 1995, the Paris Obelisk had a special 22-metre condom placed over it and, in Dorset, the Cerne Abbas giant had a condom painted on it. One peculiarity of the giant is that, in recent years, its penis has mysteriously grown in size by nearly two and a half metres. No one can work out why this is, despite research by teams of attractive young archeology students gently brushing along the surface.

Birthday –
Woody Allen
(b.1935)

In 1992, Mia Farrow described the love affair between Woody, 56, and her nineteen-year-old adopted daughter, Soon-Yi, as 'disgusting'. When she was that age, she didn't have any elderly boyfriends – her 50-year-old husband, Frank Sinatra, wouldn't allow it.

Tuesday 2

Wednesday 3

Anniversary – Tony Blair reveals he is to send his son eight miles across London to a Thatcherite opt-out school, as opposed to one of the fifty comprehensives which are nearer to his house (1994)
Margot Dunn, Head of Highbury Grove, Blair's local comprehensive, said, 'Quite frankly, I've been kicked in the teeth.' So, just a normal day teaching 3C then. Blair now has to decide whether Labour should scrap the country's 150 remaining grammar schools. But he said there was no point rushing into it – after all, his son is still only ten.

Thursday 4

Friday 5

Saturday 6

St Nicholas' Day

St Nicholas is seen as the original Santa Claus, due to his patronage of children and the custom of giving gifts on his feast day. The burial site of St Nicholas was found only recently on an island off the Turkish coast. Various clues point to it being Santa's grave: its medieval name was St Nicholas Island, it dates from the right period, and a fat man's bones are wedged half-way up the chimney.

Sunday 7

" Put off the evil hour as long as you can. "

'*Flash flood kills human pyramid.*'

'*World record attempt for number of cones on head stops earlier than expected.*'

'*Get off Mr Mellor, it's a bus.*'

IAN HISLOP'S
Bizarre
THE MAN WHO KNOWS ABOUT POP

My Live Aid pals Tina Turner and Freddie Mercury in 1996 – who I can now reveal were having an affair at the time!

It's me getting tied up with my pal David Bowie, in his Ziggy Stardust phase.

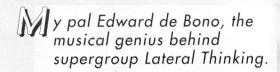

My pal Edward de Bono, the musical genius behind supergroup Lateral Thinking.

I drop in at the recording of 'Free As A Bird', another Number One hit for the pals I call 'The Fab Four'.

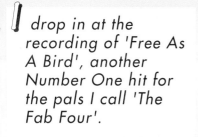

*D*own at Radio 4's Today programme, my pal Bob Marley and I debate European Monetary Union with Sir Teddy Taylor (in the radio car).

*A*nd lastly, Mick Hutchence, Paula's husband. But don't worry, we're pals really!

IAN'S TOP TEN POP CLASSICS OF ALL TIME

No.	Song	Artist	Date first entered chart
1	Gloria Laus	Bishop Theodulf of Orleans	800 AD
2	Canto Gregoriana	The Monasterio Benedictino de Santo Domingo de Silos	950 AD
3	Columba Aspexit	Abbess Hildegard of Bingen	1150
4	Ayo visto lo Mappamundi	Johannes Cornago	1455
5	Pavane Mille Regretz	Tielman Suzato	1561
6	Infelix Ego Motet	William Byrd	1580
7	Una Stravaganza dei Medici	La Pellegrina	1589
8	Nunc Dimittis	Orlando Gibbon	1620
9	Exulta Filia Sion	Claudio Monteverdi	1640
10	Don't Leave Me This Way	Jimmy Somerville	1986

ODD ONE OUT

THE QUEEN

ETON COLLEGE

THE ROYAL OPERA HOUSE

OAKFIELD OPERATIC SOCIETY

ANSWERS

Is it about the National Lottery? Because Eton College was given money, wasn't it?

To pay for new light bulbs.

Gordon, did you play the Lottery when you were presenting it?

I might have done. Who's asking?

Did you ever win?

Every week. 'Looks like 23, but it's definitely a 7'. They never twigged.

*T*he Odd One Out is Oakfield Operatic Society because, unlike the others, they don't stand to receive any money from National Lottery handouts.

*O*akfield Operatic Society is, in fact, a football club, but they changed their name in order to try and con the National Lottery into giving them a grant. Suspicions were first roused when the chorus of *Aida* started singing 'You're going to get your fucking head kicked in.'

*T*he Queen applied for Lottery money because she wanted to clean up the Tower of London. She doesn't actually play the Lottery herself, of course, because she's read that winning it can lead to the break-up of your family.

*T*he Royal Opera House received a then record payout of 58 million pounds. Lord Gowrie, chairman of the Heritage Fund, insisted that the opera was not just for the privileged few. He said, 'Any working-class person could buy a ticket'. Provided, of course, that they won the Lottery first.

*E*ton College was given Lottery cash to fund a 3 million pound, state of the art sports complex for its pupils. In face of public criticism, the Headmaster has insisted that local people will also be allowed into the fitness centre. To mop the floor and serve Pimms to parents.

The Queen's just done a Scratch-card – look at her finger.

Can I just say that the thing the Queen is wearing, that big wrapover thing, has gone out of fashion. Someone ought to go up to her and say, 'Take it off. Cut your hair short, put some Doc Martens on and you're away.'

Oh well, you got two pints anyway. Sorry, two points.

Two pints? Are we being sponsored by Unigate Dairies?

I'll have a yoghurt, if it's no trouble.

8 Monday

Anniversary – Privatisation of British Gas (1986)
Following thousands of complaints about bloated executive salaries, excessive bills and poor customer service, British Gas has been told by the regulator, Ofgas, to reduce its charges by ten per cent. The average family, struggling with its bills, will now be a whole pound-a-week better off. Which will probably be excellent news for Camelot.

Anniversary – Arthur Scargill is elected president of the National Union of Mineworkers (1981)

At the time of the miners' strike in 1984, Arthur Scargill claimed that the coal board intended axing 70,000 jobs. Coal chairman Ian McGregor said that was nonsense – and he was right. It turned out to be 170,000.

9 Tuesday

10 Wednesday

Birthday – John Birt (b.1944)

During John Birt's tenure as Director General of the BBC, there have been a number of mysterious thefts

there. Marmaduke Hussey, the 70-year-old BBC Chairman, was amazed when his secretary told him that his video had been stolen from his office. He'd always assumed it was a teasmade. Comedian Bob Monkhouse had a notebook containing his finest jokes stolen from a BBC office and John Birt himself had a £200 mahogany toilet seat stolen. Police say they have nothing to go on.*

* Thanks, Bob.

11 Thursday

Anniversary – abdication of Edward VIII

The Duke of Windsor, formally King Edward VIII, was the subject of a documentary which alleged that, as a Nazi sympathiser, he toured a concentration camp and an SS training centre, and also advised Hitler that only 'continued and severe bombing of England' would make this country see sense. And to think members of the Royal Family are unpopular nowadays because they've got big bottoms or shag rugby players.

12 Friday

Birthday – Will Carling (b.1965)

Not surprisingly, when Will Carling's affair with Princess Diana became public knowledge, the press started disinterring Carling's previous relationships. While on tour with England in New Zealand, he wrote to one girlfriend, Victoria Taylor-Jackson, saying, 'I came up with another rather erotic idea this morning, which I shall put into practice some time on Monday!' Must have come as a bit of a shock to the All Blacks' fly-half.

13 Saturday

14 Sunday

❝ Every proverb has its opposite. ❞

I'm sure the others went in here last year.

Oven ready, turkey.

Going anywhere nice for Christmas?

By-pass scheme has design fault.

That's the Cerne Abbas giant and they're just touching it up.

Is this a gravel path or are you just pleased to see me?

15 Monday

16 Tuesday

Birthday – Ludwig van Beethoven (b.1770)
Beethoven's 'Ode to Joy' was the BBC's controversial choice as theme music for their Euro 96 football coverage. For the benefit of their readers, the ever-helpful *Daily Express* pictured Beethoven as he would have looked had he played for Germany.

Obviously Ludwig went to the same hairdresser as Kevin Keegan.

17 Wednesday

18 Thursday

Anniversary – The first lottery jackpot winner fights to cling on to his anonymity (1994)

All we know is he's Asian and he doesn't want anyone to know who he is or where he lives. So it must be Salman Rushdie.

This bloke is now the fifteen-hundredth richest person in the United Kingdom. Sandwiched neatly, apparently, between Noel Edmunds and the Queen Mother.

Must have been a hell of a party.

Friday 19

Birthday – Eamonn Andrews (1922)

The original host of *This Is Your Life*, Eamonn Andrews owed much of his early success to TV producer, Gordon Reece the man who also advised Margaret Thatcher on her TV image. According to Reece, 'It's important not to wear a lot of fuss on television. Scoop necklines are out. Go easy on lots of jewellery.' Advice which completely changed Eamonn Andrews' career.

Saturday 20

Sunday 21

Anniversary – Premiere of the first feature-length cartoon, Walt Disney's *Snow White and the Seven Dwarfs* (1937)

In 1993, a pantomime featuring the seven dwarfs was censured by Hull Council for fear of offending short people and an Islington theatre banned Tinkerbell from a production of *Peter Pan*, to avoid embarassing references to fairies. In folklore, fairies are described as 'beings of diminutive stature, who cheerfully intermeddle in people's lives'. But if you want to call Noel Edmunds a fairy, that's entirely between you and your lawyers.

Despite its wholesome image, when the Disney film of *Snow White* first came out, the post-production party quickly turned into a drunken orgy – with everything from unnatural acts Goofy-style, to having a straight Donald.

 No more proverbs for me, no more hackneyed old phrases. I'm making a fresh start.

22 Monday

23 Tuesday

24 Wednesday
1 shopping day left till Christmas

25 Thursday
Birthday – Jesus Christ (b.0)

A goodly man whose suffering on this earth included getting only one set of presents every year.

Birthday – Damien Hirst (b.1955)

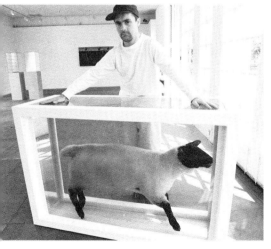

At London's Serpentine Gallery, Damien Hirst's controversial sculpture of a dead sheep floating in a tank of formaldehyde, which had already sold for £25,000, was vandalised when a bottle of ink was poured into it. The most likely culprits were animal rights activists – after a previous Hirst exhibition, they had left a huge pile of dog mess on the gallery steps; it should have been cleared away immediately but, owing to a misunderstanding, was sold to an American for £50,000.

Friday 26

Saturday 27
Anniversary – Britain's Sex Discrimination Act comes into force (1975)

In 1996, the Equal Opportunities Commission reported that, for the first time, more men than women were complaining about sexual discrimination in the jobs market. This followed the move by men into traditionally female-dominated positions, such as nurse, secretary, receptionist and Prime Minister.

One female executive who was looking for a new receptionist turned away a bricklayer who had applied. She said she didn't want to be caught looking at his cleavage every time his back was turned.

Sunday 28
Birthday – Roy Hattersley (b.1932)

Monday 29

Tuesday 30

Wednesday 31
Anniversary – At the age of 89, Barbara Cartland is made a Dame on the New Year's Honours List (1990)

In a recent interview, Dame Barbara attributes her enduring good looks to a Danish body cream called 'Flame'. She says, 'My body is exactly like that of an 18-year-old girl'. The 18-year-old girl in question has since committed suicide.

❝ Happy New Year. ❞

Useless Information

Conversion Table

1 pint = 0.683 litres
2 pints = 1.366 litres
3 pints = 2.9 no, hang on, 3. 1 er, no, why did I have three pints..?
10 pints = yerfugga bloody gafugovv

4 gills = 1 pint
0 gills = dead fish

Temperature Conversion Table For Old People

Degrees	Temperature For Old People
0	'Ooh, isn't it cold.'
10	'Ooh, isn't it cold.'
15	'Ooh, isn't it cold.'
35	'Ooh, I might take my overcoat off.'

Time In Other Parts Of The World

France	Plus 1 hour
Japan	Plus 9 hours
Russia	Minus about 30 years

Useless Phone Numbers

Belfast Tourist Office – 01876 540245
Wimbledon FC Advance Ticket Office – 0181 673 4089
Scottish Conservatives, Membership Hotline – 0800 777845
Mrs G Northover, 3 The Mews, Cleethorpes – 01654 710439

True Facts, but still useless

WORLD'S MOST PROLIFIC PRODUCER OF NUTMEG	*Grenada*
LETTERS NOT USED IN SPELLING THE NAMES OF THE STATES OF AMERICA	*q*
OCEAN CLOSEST TO THE WORLD AVERAGE OCEAN SIZE	*Indian*
WORLD'S BIGGEST CONSUMER OF LEA & PERRINS WORCESTER SAUCE	*El Salvador*
NUMBER ONE HIT THAT INCLUDED IN ITS LYRICS THE TITLE OF THE RECORD THAT KNOCKED IT OFF THE NUMBER ONE SPOT	*'Bohemian Rhapsody'* *(Mamma Mia)*

At-a-glance Year Planner For 1998

January 1 – Put up Year Planner
January 2 – Stop bothering to fill in Year Planner

The Most Useless Information of All

Published by BBC Books
an imprint of BBC Worldwide Publishing Limited
Woodlands, 80 Wood Lane
London W12 0TT

First published 1996

© Hat Trick Productions Limited 1996
Design and typesetting © BBC

ISBN: 0 563 38783 1

Design by Harry Green
Special photography by Stuart Wood
Illustrations by Karen Cochrane, Tony Coles, Hardlines, Fiona Plummer, and Technical Art Services. Back cover illustrations by Triffic Films.

Printed and bound in Great Britain by Butler & Tanner Limited, Frome, Somerset
Colour separations by Radstock Repro Limited, Midsomer Norton, Avon
Cover printed by Lawrence Allen Limited, Western-super-Mare, Avon

BBC Books would like to thank the following for providing photographs and for permission to reproduce copyright material. While every effort has been made to trace and acknowledge all copyright holders, we would like to apologise should there have been any errors or omissions. AFP, AirWair, All Action, Angler's Mail, Aquarius, C Arron, Assignments, Associated Press, R Bamber, Bamaby's, Bridgeman Art Library, G Calton, Cambridge Town Crier, Camera Press, Caters News Agency, Corbis, A Cullen, A Davidson, Mary Evans, Express Synd., Financial Times, John Frost, P Grover, The Guardian, Hulton Getty, Independent Synd., Kobal Collection, S Lock, D Mansell, Mirror Synd., Alastair Muir, News International, Oakfield Football Club, PA News, Paramount Pictures, P Payne, K Phillips, Planet Earth, Popperfoto, C Postlethwaite, Rex Features, D Sandison, Science Photo Library, Scottish Daily Record, Ski Club of GB, Solo Synd., South West News Services, Frank Spooner, Telegraph Group, University of Zimbabwe, UPPA, Westminster Abbey, Westmoreland Gazette, Stuart Wood, Woodlands Animation.

KEY PEOPLE

▲ Sue Harmer
⚷ Nick Martin
☎ John Ryan
✈ Toby Stevens
✍ Anna Ottewill
⚲ Harry Green
☎ Susannah Playfair

```
0          100 miles
|----------|
0          150 km
```

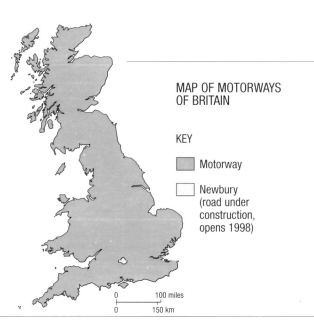

MAP OF MOTORWAYS OF BRITAIN

KEY

▨ Motorway

☐ Newbury (road under construction, opens 1998)

```
0          100 miles
|----------|
0          150 km
```